Assurance

Dedicated to the life and memory of
Cardinal Basil Hume, O.S.B.
(1923–1999)

Assurance

AN ANTHOLOGY

Edited by Michael Seed

CONTINUUM

London and New York

Continuum

The Tower Building	370 Lexington Avenue
11 York Road	New York
London SE1 7NX	NY 10017–6503

© 2000 Continuum International Publishing
Text © 2000 in this arrangement Michael Seed

British Library Cataloguing-in-Publication Data
A catalogue record for this book is available from the British Library.

| ISBN | 0–8264–4987–5 |
| ISBN | 0–8264–4357–0 |

Designed and typeset by Ben Cracknell Studios
Printed and bound in Great Britain by Biddles Ltd, Guildford and King's Lynn

List of Contributors

HRH The Duchess of Kent

Jonathan Aitken	Former politician
Maria Aitken	Actress
Mohamed Al Fayed	Owner of Harrods and chairman of Fulham Football Club
Lord Alton	Human rights campaigner and professor of citzenship
Peter Alliss	Broadcaster
Lady Astor	Former model and widow of Lord Astor of Hever
Zaki Badawi	Principal, Muslim College, London
Beryl Bainbridge	Novelist
Robin Baird-Smith	Publisher
Lady Elizabeth Basset	Editor, *Love is my Meaning* (1973), former Lady in Waiting to Queen Elizabeth the Queen Mother
Stanley Baxter	Comedian and actor
John Bayley	Author and widower of Dame Iris Murdoch
Sister Wendy Beckett	Author, broadcaster and art expert
Tony Benn	Politician
Conrad Black	Newspaper proprietor
Tony Blair	UK Prime Minister
Sir Louis Blom-Cooper	Barrister and campaigner for law reform

Michael Blakemore	Actor and director
Rabbi Lionel Blue	Rabbi, author and broadcaster
Rory Bremner	Comedian
Cherie Booth	Barrister
Noel Botham	Author and journalist
Nico Brenninkmeyer	Businesssman and philanthropist
Stephen Brenninkmeyer	Businesssman and philanthropist
Sir George Bull	Chairman, J. Sainsbury plc
Gay Byrne	Broadcaster
Sholto Byrnes	Journalist
Lord Callaghan	Former British Prime Minister
George Carey	Archbishop of Canterbury
Lord Carter	Government Chief Whip, House of Lords
Barbara Cartland	Author
Edward Idris Cassidy	Christian Unity, The Vatican
Richard Chartres	Bishop of London
Hillary Clinton	US First Lady and candidate for the US Senate
Sir Terence Conran	Style guru
Lord Clyde	Law Lord
Sir Simon Cooper	Master of Royal Household
Jilly Cooper	Novelist
Lady Anthea Craigmyle	Philanthropist
Nirj Deva	Politician
John Dewe Matthews	Artist
Barry Fantoni	Writer, broadcaster and cartoonist

Frederick Forsyth	Novelist
Frank Field	Politician
Sir Ronnie Flanagan	Chief Constable, RUC
Sir George Gardiner	Writer and politician
John Gowans	General of the Salvation Army
Archbishop Gregorios	Greek Orthodox Archbishop of Great Britain
Sir Charles Guthrie	Chief of the Defence Staff
William Hague	Leader of Her Majesty's Opposition
Alison Halford	Former police officer and Member of the Welsh Assembly
Neil Hamilton	Former Member of Parliament
Georgina Hammick	Author
Sir Edward Heath	Former British Prime Minister
Lord Harris of High Cross	Founder, Institute of Economic Affairs
James Herbert	Novelist
Gopichand Hinduja	Businessman and philanthropist
Richard Ingrams	Writer, broadcaster and former Editor of *Private Eye*
Eric James	Anglican priest and broadcaster
Sir Edward Jones	Gentleman Usher of the Black Rod
HRH Princess Michael of Kent	
Neil Kinnock	Politician, European Commissioner
Linda Lader	Wife of US ambassador
Philip Lader	US Ambassador to Great Britain
John Le Carré	Novelist
Patrick Lichfield	Photographer

Magnus Linklater	Journalist and political commentator
Countess of Longford	Author
Earl of Longford	Author and politician
Veronica Maclean	Author and widow of Sir Fitzroy McLean
John Major	Former British Prime Minister
Terry Major-Ball	Author, columnist and brother of John Major
Lady Menuhin	Widow of Lord Menhuin
Ann Monsarrat	Author and widow of Nicholas Monsarrat
Viscount Montgomery of El Alamein	Businessman and specialist in Latin American affairs
Sir John Mortimer	Novelist and barrister
Cormac Murphy-O'Connor	Archbishop of Westminster
Sir Angus Ogilvy	Businessman and husband of HRH Princess Alexandra
Matthew Parris	Writer and broadcaster
Lord Owen	Politician
Christopher Patten	European Commissioner
Earl of Perth	Peer of the realm and philanthropist
Lord Pilkington	Peer and former High Master of St Paul's School
Tim Pigott-Smith	Actor
Prince Rainier of Monaco	Sovereign of Monaco
Olga Polizzi	Businesswoman
Sir Cliff Richard	Singer
Piers Paul Read	Novelist, writer
Lord Rix	Peer, actor and philanthropist

Tom Robinson	Musician
Lord Runcie	Former Archbishop of Canterbury
Lord Rossmore	Irish Peer
Rabbi Jonathan Sacks	Chief Rabbi
Sir Jimmy Savile	Broadcaster
Roger Scruton	Philosopher and author
Paul Scofield	Actor
Ned Sherrin	Broadcaster and author
Muriel Spark	Novelist
Earl Spencer	Peer of the realm and brother of the late Princess of Wales
Sir Sigmund Sternberg	Businessman and philanthropist
Sir John Stevens	Commissioner of the Metropolitan Police
Peter Stothard	Editor of *The Times*
Edward Stourton	Broadcaster
Joan Sutherland	Opera singer
Kiri Te Kanawa	Opera singer
Sir John Templeton	Businessman and philanthropist
Baroness Thatcher	Former British Prime Minister
Neil Tennant	Musician
Archbishop Desmond Tutu	Former Archbishop of Capetown and Nobel Peace Prize Winner
Chad Varah	Founder of the Samaritans
Sir Dennis Walters	Former Member of Parliament
Baroness Warnock	Philosopher
Lord Weatherill	Former Speaker of the House of Commons
Ann Widdecombe	Shadow Home Secretary and novelist

John Wilkins	Editor of *The Tablet*
Baroness Williams	Politician
Sir Peregrine Worsthorne	Political journalist and former Editor of *The Sunday Telegraph*
Philip Ziegler	Author and publisher

Acknowledgements

I wish to thank Daniel Bouquet at Continuum for his tireless energy and patience in keeping my mind on the project. I am also indebted to David Hayden, Ben Pitcher and to Continuum's Chairman, Philip Sturrock, for their wisdom and practical assistance.

There are many others to thank, but my special thanks goes to Benjamin Harnwell who so generously gave his time to the exacting task of collating and preparing this work.

PALACE GREEN
LONDON W8 4PU

In this turbulent world we are all in need of re-assurance. In the pages of this book you will find words which have encouraged, comforted and inspired many.

It is hoped that these same words will bring great peace of mind to the readers - both in everyday life and in times of anxiety.

Katharine Kent

<u>The Duchess of Kent</u>

Preface

I remember being taken by my grandmother to school for the first time and being left feeling anxious and abandoned in the playground. I comforted myself with the thought that, God willing, I would make it back home safely where, after a hug, all would be well. I soon realised that I would go back the next day and might just be able to cope with school.

From the vantage of adulthood the problems of most five-year-olds can seem slight and transient. In comparison, our grown-up troubles can seem permanent and intractable and at times create a deep need for comfort and encouragement. This book is a collection of a number of texts that have inspired people with assurance. The contributors range widely across public life; indeed some have been at odds with each other, but they all share the common experience of need in a time of difficulty. The need to carry on through conflict, tribulation and indignity to inner peace, contentment and assurance. I am indebted to all of them and hope that this book will provide a source of comfort for those enduring suffering and seeking spiritual peace.

I am greatly indebted to the Duchess of Kent for her kindness in writing the foreword to this anthology. The Duchess is a dearly loved lady whose actions and words have always given me, and countless others, assurance.

The royalties from this book will assist the work of both The Passage day and night centre for the homeless, which was founded by the late Cardinal Hume in 1980, and the Franciscan Friars of the Atonement, a religious order founded to further ecumenical and inter-faith understanding.

Michael Seed

Petertide 2000

From: Jonathan Aitken

May 31 2000

Dear Father Seed,

Thank you for your recent letter about your plans to edit **An Anthology of Assurance**. I am honored and delighted to offer you a contribution to this collection of passages on assurance.

One of the many reasons why I am so willing to co-operate with you is that the similar work you mentioned in your letter 'An Anthology of Assurance' was one of my favourite books in prison. I often lent it to other prisoners who like me, found Lady Elizabeth Bassett's selections moving and inspiring.

May I wish you God's blessing for your work on **An Anthology of Assurance** and on your wider ministry.

Yours sincerely

Jonathan Aitken

Jonathan Aitken

From:
A Serious and Devout Call to a Holy Life
by William Law.

If anyone would tell you the shortest, surest way
to all perfection and happiness, he must tell you to make
it a rule to yourself to thank and praise God for everything that
happens to you. For it is certain that whatever seeming calamity
happens to you, if you thank and praise God for it, you
turn it into a blessing.

A Prayer of Saint Ignatius Loyola

Take Lord and receive all my liberty, all my will, all
my understanding, everything I have and possess. For you
gave these things to me and to you I gladly return them.
Only dear Lord in your mercy grant me your peace
and your grace for these are enough for me.

MARIA AITKEN

29th May 2000

Dear Father Michael, This is a belated response to your letter and I'm sorry. I live in New York part of the year and my mail often lingers for weeks in the wrong city. Or so I tell people.

A very short passage from James Agate's _Ego 3_ has often comforted me when people die too young. He transcribed it from the "In Memoriam" column of _The Times_.

"All the beautiful time is yours for always, for it is life that takes away, changes and spoils so often — not death, which is really the warden and not the thief of our treasures".

I hope this will do for your anthology.

All good wishes,

Maria Aitken

BY APPOINTMENT TO
HER MAJESTY THE QUEEN
SUPPLIERS OF PROVISIONS
AND HOUSEHOLD GOODS
HARRODS LTD. LONDON

BY APPOINTMENT TO
H.R.H. THE DUKE OF EDINBURGH
OUTFITTERS
HARRODS LTD. LONDON

BY APPOINTMENT TO
H.M. QUEEN ELIZABETH THE QUEEN MOTHER
SUPPLIERS OF CHINA, GLASS
AND FANCY GOODS
HARRODS LTD. LONDON

BY APPOINTMENT TO
H.R.H. THE PRINCE OF WALES
OUTFITTERS AND SADDLERS
HARRODS LTD. LONDON

HARRODS LIMITED, KNIGHTSBRIDGE, LONDON SW1X 7XL • TELEPHONE 020-7730 1234 • FAX 020-7581 0470 • www.harrods.com

Chairman's Office

8 May 2000

Dear Michael

Thank you for your letter of 17th April. I am delighted to help you develop your fund raising activities as an editor for such worthy causes!

As you know I am a Muslim – although not a very strict one – but I believe we are all God's children. I have read with interest the sacred texts of the world's great religions and it seems to me they have a common theme – that we should care for our fellow man. I know that you devote your life to this and I try to do my best each day.

The text I have chosen is for that precious moment when a new day begins. It is a prayer from the Holy Koran which I have found of great comfort in bad times – a wonderful reminder of God's love:

**By the forenoon, bright,
and the night
when dark and quiet,
your Lord has not abandoned you
and does not despise you.
Surely hereafter is better for you,
than what was before.
And your Lord will surely give to you,
and you will be pleased.
Did God not find you orphaned
and provide you refuge?
And find you wandering,
and guide you?
And find you needy,
and enrich you?
So do not oppress the orphan,
or refuse the one who seeks.
And tell of the bounty of your Lord.**
(Translation by Thomas Cleary)

I wish you every success in your latest venture.

Yours sincerely

**M. Al Fayed
Chairman**

Registered in London No 30209 Registered Office 87/135 Brompton Road Knightsbridge London SW1X 7XL

Professor the Lord Alton of Liverpool

House of Lords
London SW1A 0PW

May 2000.

Dear Father Michael,

Thank you very much for your letter about Assurance. I have put together some of the texts which give me encouragement and I hope others will also find assurance in them.

In her address to the United Nations Mother Teresa of Calcutta said "Life is the most beautiful gift of God. That is why it is so painful to see what is happening today in so many places around the world; life is being deliberately destroyed by war, by violence, by abortion..." She joined forced with Pope John Paul II in countering what he later called "the culture of death." In a world in which human life is turned into a commodity and is exploited and degraded at every turn, here are two rare but authentic voices calling for justice.

In 1979, when the prospect of peace in Northern Ireland seemed an impossibility I felt very moved by the sight of Pope John Paul II standing on the Hill of Slane, where so many centuries before St.Patrick had lit his Pascal Fire, calling for reconciliation and peace. He urged his listeners to redouble their efforts to "light up the darkness of these years of trial."

Speaking directly to those engaged in terrorism he said: "I appeal to you, in language of passionate pleading. On my knees I beg you to turn away from the paths of violence and to return to the ways of peace. You may claim to seek justice. I too believe in justice and seek justice. But violence only delays the day of justice. Violence destroys the work of justice. Further violence will only drag down to ruin the land you claim to love and the values you claim to cherish. In the name of God I beg you: return to Christ, who died so that men might live in forgiveness and peace. He is waiting for you, longing for each one of you to come to him so that He may say to each of you: your sins are forgiven; go in peace." As he would do again in Jerusalem in the year 2000, the Pope called for pardon and for peace.

"I came to Drogheda today on a great mission of peace and reconciliation. I come as a pilgrim of peace. To Catholics, to Protestants, my message is peace and love. May no Irish Protestant think that the pope is an enemy, a danger or a threat. My desire is that instead Protestants would see in me a friend and a brother in Christ. Do not lose trust that this visit of mine may be fruitful, that this voice of mine may be listened to. And even if it were not listened to, let history record that at a difficult moment in the experience of the people of Ireland, the bishop of Rome set foot in your land, that he was with you and prayed with you for peace and reconciliation, for the victory of love and justice over hatred and violence".

Director: **The Foundation for Citizenship, Liverpool John Moores University**
Roscoe Court, 4 Rodney Street, Liverpool L1 2TZ

Professor the Lord Alton of Liverpool

House of Lords
London SW1A 0PW

Cardinal Basil Hume's deep spiritual insights have also given me and many another great assurance as we wrestle with our weakness. He spoke to the hearts of those seeking reconciliation with God and struggling to find peace as they prepared for death. In 1984 he wrote this, in "To Be A Pilgrim":

"As we approach the last bit of the journey there are days when we fear that we face an unknown, unpredictable, future. That is a common experience. But do not worry; because the time comes when we no longer carry heavy bags and all those possessions. We shall travel through the cold, grey light of a bleak English morning into God's Spring and Summer; into His light and warmth.

"This day you will be with me in paradise"(Luke 23:43).This day will inevitably come for each one of us, we do not know when. But it most surely will come and what a joy it will be when we hear the words: "This day you will be with me in paradise." We must move in our spiritual lives from thinking of death as the great enemy and begin to uncertain think about "this day" as the one when we shall be going home, the one for which we were made and for which the whole of our lives is the preparation.

Life is indeed a pilgrimage as we walk each day closer towards its end which is the vision of God. We are made for that and life is a preparation for the moment when we move from this situation into eternal happiness. Joy and sorrow, agony and ecstasy, pain and well-being: they walk hand in hand up that hill which is called Calvary. But beyond it to a place where there is no more death, no sin, no pain, only empty tombs and life everlasting."

But when discomforted by doubt, or seeking solace, perhaps one of the greatest friends is the fourteenth century Catholic writer, Thomas a Kempis. I was not surprised when James Mawdsley, the young Catholic human rights activist jailed for seventeen years by the Burmese military, asked for "The Imitation of Christ" and the Bible as the two books which they initially allowed him:

"Do dilligently what you do; toil faithfully in my vineyard; I will be

your wages. Write, read, sing, weep, be silent, pray, endure adversities

manfully; eternal life is worth all these conflicts and greater. Peace

will come on one day, which is known to the Lord. And it will be

neither day nor night, as we know it at this time, but light unending,

brightness without end, established peace and carefree rest...death shall

be hurled down, salvation shall not fail, there will be no anxiety, blessed

joy, sweet and beauteous friendship."

In writing may I express my continued admiration for the work which is undertaken by The Passage and I hope that the anthology will raise substantial funds to help them in their crucial work providing a refuge for London's homeless people.

With good wishes,

Yours sincerely,

David Alton.

David Alton.

Director: **The Foundation for Citizenship, Liverpool John Moores University**
Roscoe Court, 4 Rodney Street, Liverpool L1 2TZ

British Broadcasting Corporation   Television Centre Wood Lane London W12 7RJ Telephone 0181 225 6401 Fax 0181 749 3560

B B C Production

Television, Golf Production Office

17 April 2000

Dear *Father Michael*.

In response to your note regarding AN ANTHOLOGY OF ASSURANCE, I offer you the following:

"I would be true for there are those who trust me.   I would be pure for there are those who care.   I would be strong for there is much to suffer.   I would be brave for there is much to dare.   I would be friend of all, the foe, the friendless.   I would be giving and forget the gift.   I would be humble for I know my weakness.   I would look up and laugh and love and live."

I hope these few words are worthy.   They have been of comfort to me on several occasions over the past 20 years.

Sincerely

Peter Alliss

Long ago, in the East, it was common practice for carpet-weavers to sit in the market place working away at their looms. They wove wonderful pictures and patterns into their carpets, but while the work was in progress, only the weaver could see them. Anyone looking at the back of the carpet would have seen only a very untidy-looking hotch-potch of colours, but the weaver knew exactly what he was doing. Someone wrote a verse which likens God to the weaver, working out his design on the canvas of our lives. It goes like this:

Then shall I know

Not till the loom is silent and the shuttles cease to fly
Shall God unroll the canvas and reveal the reason why.
The dark threads are as needful in the weaver's skilful hand
As the threads of gold and silver in the patterns he has planned.

Traditional

In Isaiah, chapter 55 we read that God's thoughts are not our thoughts and his ways are not our ways. When we encounter things which we cannot understand, then we need to remind ourselves of the words of the Psalmist: 'This God – his way is perfect' (Ps. 18:30).

It is like looking at the back of a tapestry: one can see that there is a design but cannot discern what it is. It is only when we have left the world that we shall be able to see the beauty of the other side, and then we shall understand.

Teilhard de Chardin

Tuesley Manor

2. V. 00

Dear Father Michael.

Thank you for asking me to contribute to **AN ANTHOLOGY OF ASSURANCE.** The text which immediately springs to mind is from *Le Milieu Divin* by Teilhard de Chardin which goes as follows:-

God, in all that is most living and incarnate in Him, is not far away from us, altogether apart from the world we see, touch, hear, smell and taste about us. Rather He awaits us every instant in our action, in the work of the moment. There is a sense in which He is at the tip of my pen, my spade, my brush, my needle - of my heart and of my thought. By pressing the stroke, the line, or the stitch, on which I am engaged, to its ultimate natural finish, I shall lay hold of that last end towards which my inner-most will tends. Like those formidable physical forces which man contrives to dis-cipline so as to make them perform operations of prodigious delicacy, so the tremendous power of the divine attraction is focused on our frail desires and micro-scopic intents without breaking their point. It sur-animates; hence it neither disturbs anything nor stifles anything. It sur-animates; hence it introduces a higher principle of unity into our spiritual life, the specific effect of which is - depending upon the point of view one adopts - either to make man's endeavour holy, or to give the Christian life the full flavour of humanity.

Ever with love

Bronwen Astor

Principal
Professor M A Zaki Badawi
Al-Alimiyyah (Al-Azhar) PhD. (London)

THE MUSLIM COLLEGE
20/22 Creffield Road, London W5 3RP.

28th June 2000

Date:

Dear Father Michael

Here is the supplication attributed to 'Abd al-Qadir al-Jilani which never fails to move me every time I read or recite it.

> **I have naught but my destitution**
>   **To plead for me with Thee.**
> **And in my poverty I put forward that destitution as**
>   **my plea.**
> **I have no power save to knock at Thy door,**
> **And if I be turned away, at what door shall I**
>   **knock?**
> **Or on whom shall I call, crying his name,**
> **If Thy generosity is refused to Thy destitute one?**
> **Far be it from Thy generosity to drive the disobedient**
>   **one to despair!**
> **Generosity is more freehanded than that.**
> **In lowly wretchedness I have come to Thy door**
> **Knowingly that degradation there finds help.**
> **In full abandon I put my trust in Thee,**
> **Stretching out my hands to Thee, a pleading**
>   **beggar.**

Yours sincerely

M.A. Zaki Badawi

To the Franciscan Friars,

Many years ago I bought a second hand paperback entitled
Mediaeval Latin Lyrics, translated by Helen Waddell and first
published in 1929.

There was one poem in particular, by Venantius Fortunatus,
that I found haunting, and still do. Having learnt it by
heart so long ago, I often recite it to myself, for, with its
reminder of mortality, it fits both good times and bad. I
know nothing about Greek literature, nor do I understand
Latin, but the names give me comfort, and Waddell gives the
Latin text beside the translation, the first line being,
Tempora lapsa volant, fugitivis fallimur horis....

Time that is fallen is flying, we are fooled by the passing
hours...
Likeness is none between us, but we go to the self same end.
The foot that has crossed the threshold shall no man
withdraw again.
....What help in the arms of the fighters? Hector, and
vengeful Achilles

Fallen,Ajax is fallen,whose shield was the wall of Greece.

Beauty,beauty passeth,Astur the fairest is fallen ,

Low Hippolytus lieth,Adonis liveth no more.

And where are the songs of the singers? Silent for all

their sweetness.

Small joy to be won in prolonging the notes of the song.

Even as the moments are dying,the present is flying,

The dice are snatched from our hands and the game is done.

Naught but the deeds of the just live on in a flower that is

 blessed;

Sweetness comes from the grave where a good man lieth dead.

With all good wishes

Beryl Bainbridge

Camden Town. London, April 2000

CONTINUUM
CONTINUUM

The Continuum International Publishing Group Ltd
The Tower Building 11 York Road London SE1 7NX
Telephone: 020 7922 0880

Dea Michael,

Low Spirits

Foston, 16 February 1820

Dear Lady Georgiana,

…Nobody has suffered more from low spirits than I have done- so I feel for you.

1st Live as well as you dare

2nd. Go into the shower-bath with a small quantity of water at a temperature low enough to give you a slight sensation of cold, 75 or 80 degrees.

3rd. Amusing books.

4th. Short views of human life- not further than dinner or tea.

5th. Be as busy as you can.

6th. See as much as you can of those friends who respect and like you.

7th. And of those acquaintances who amuse you.

8th. Make no secret of low spirits to your friends but talk of them freely- they are always worse for dignified concealment.

9th. Attend to the effects tea and coffee produce upon you.

10th. Compare your lot with that of other people.

12th. Don`t expect too much from human life- a sorry business at the best.

LONDON   NEW YORK

Registered in England No. 3833148

13th Do good, and endeavour to please everybody of every degree.

14th. Be as much as you can in the open air without fatigue.

15th. Make the room where you commonly sit gay and pleasant.

16th. Struggle by little and little against idleness.

17th. Don`t be too severe upon yourself, or underrate yourself, but do yourself justice.

18th. Keep good blazing fires.

19th. Be firm and constant in the exercise of rational religion.

20th Believe me, dear Lady Georgiana, …

Sydney Smith
To Lady Georgiana Morpeth

This has often helped me. I hope your book makes a lot of money for your charities.

Yours,

Robin Baird-Smith

July 5th

Dear Father Michael

Thank you so much for your kind letter.

I am so delighted to hear you are compiling an anthology. I think Love is My Meaning has met a need in these hectic times when people don't have time to read long books Its contents came from other men's writings all of which brought me comfort in my darkest days

I think one of the texts that has meant
a great deal to me comes from
Gerard Manley Hopkins.
"We all have this one work to do
To let God's Glory through".
It seems to make all one's
rather pathetic efforts so infinitely
worth while

Wilt very best wishes and please
let me know when your Anthology is
published.
Again many thanks for all you say
& Yours ever Elizabeth Basset

STANLEY BAXTER

25 · IV · 00

Dear Father Michael,
Thank you for your letter
of April 7th. The enclosed piece might not
be at all what you are hoping for, and I
will quite understand if you decide not
to use it.

Yours sincerely

Stanley Baxter

I hope I will be forgiven for not quoting a comforting text, but instead recounting a happening that inspired me.

On the death of one of my closest friends in Glasgow, I went North for the funeral. When the clergyman officiating came on to the little rostrum of the crematorium, the lady next to me said, "Oh! That's a Roman Catholic priest, I can tell from the way he's dressed." We both knew that our friend Arthur was not of that persuasion and wondered what form the service would take. Well, it wasn't a religious service at all. The priest explained that he was officiating as a friend of Arthur's and not in his usual capacity. He went on to say that he knew Arthur (like myself) was not a believer and didn't wish to violate his wishes by performing a Christian service. He then went on to speak of Arthur in such moving terms; of his generosity and kindness to all who passed his way, that for the first time in my life I felt tears well up at a funeral service.

It is so painful for anyone who does not subscribe to the belief in an afterlife to listen to a Christian service with its assurances of life everlasting. To us it seems wildly improbable! Yet here was a priest whose views on the subject were – by conviction and calling – so different from Arthur's and mine, coming to speak of Arthur's life with such love – and promising us, as he had promised Arthur, that no religious text would be invoked.

How generous, how admirable. If it didn't quite make me a convert, it gave me assurance that even a Catholic priest's devotion to a friend could rise above dogma. Maybe it always does........................

Stanley Baxter

St. Catherine's College · Oxford · OX1 3UJ

Dear Father Michael, one of these
will surprise you! — the passage on how
he came back to the church in Beverley
Nichols The Fool Hath Said. Father
Thames's address in Barbara Pym's
A Glass of Blessings ("this may surprise
you' is the comic Keynote...) & the
death of Marcia at the end of
Quartet in Autumn. v. moving & d
uplifting. Some good I hope?
    All good luck for your project.
        John Bayley

John Bayley

A Glass of Blessings

My friends,' he began, 'how very glad I am to see so many of you here this evening. As some of you know, I am shortly leaving for a holiday in Italy. There seems something a little unsuitable, does there not, about a clergyman going for a holiday in Italy in these difficult days? When we hear about such a thing perhaps we remember our *Barchester Towers* – the older ones among us that is.' He seemed to be looking at Sir Denbigh Grote and Miss Prideaux as he said this, perhaps feeling that they alone were old enough to have read Trollope. We think of Canon Vesey Stanhope and his villa on the shores of Lake Como – or was it Maggiore? Not Garda, I think – I forget the details. As I was saying, we remember that, and it might be thought that there was a parallel there.' Father Thames paused for laughter, which came a little uncertainly, though one elderly choirman clapped his hands and guffawed perhaps too heartily for such a gathering. Father Thames held up his hand and went on, '*But*, and this will surprise you, who can say that there might not be something in it after all?' His hearers were now mystified and waited his next words with considerable interest. I am an old man,' he went on. 'Oh yes, you may protest and say that you have seen older priests carrying out their duties perfectly capably – indeed Father Fosdick, who has sometimes assisted us here at holiday times, is nearly ninety, and a great joy it has always been to have him with us – but I have passed my threescore years and ten, and it may be that the time has come for me to make way for a younger man. *It may be.*' He paused impressively, then went on in a more confidential tone, 'I was talking to the Bishop at luncheon the other day – he knows full well the rigours of this parish. Now *you* know, most of you, that I have friends – kind friends they are – near Siena whom I visit every year for rest and refreshment, to enable me to *carry on*, as it were. *Well*' – there was another impressive pause – 'what do you think? A villa has fallen vacant there! *Da affittare!* A small villa with just four bedrooms and a delightful garden – the Villa Cenerentola. What a delightful name that is, and perhaps not altogether inappropriate.'

Quartet in Autumn

The young doctor bent over Marcia. He didn't like the look of her at all – indeed she was the kind of patient one didn't like the look of at the best of times. Luckily Mr Strong was still around and it took only a minute to get him back again. He had been very concerned about Miss Ivory and would want to be around if anything happened.

Mr Strong was still wearing that green tie – was it the same tie or did he just like the colour green? It had a small, close design on it. His rather bushy eyebrows were drawn together over his grey eyes in a frown. He always seemed to be frowning – had she done something wrong? Not eaten enough, perhaps? His eyes seemed to bore into her – the piercing eyes of the surgeon, did people say that? No, it was rather the surgeon's hands that people noticed and commented on, like the hands of a pianist when, at a concert, people tried to sit where they could see the pianist's hands. But in a sense the surgeon was just as much of an artist, that beautiful neat scar ... Marcia remembered what her mother used to say, how she would never let the surgeon's knife touch er body. how ridiculous that seemed when one considered Mr Strong ... Marcia smiled and the frown left his face and he seemed to be smiling back at her.

The chaplain, on his way to visit Miss Ivory, was told that he was too late. 'Miss Ivory's gone, passed on ...' the words rang in his head like a television advertisement jingle, but he prayed for the repose of her soul and nerved himself for the meeting with her next of kin and other relatives. But the man he eventually saw didn't seem to be any relation at all, just a 'friend' who was stepping into the breach, as it were. Somebody who had worked in the same office. Rather surprisingly, he held the view that there was nothing to reproach oneself with for not having been able to prevent death when, for the Christian, it was so much to be desired. Everything concerning Miss Ivory was settled with calm efficiency, without recriminations and certainly without tears, and that was a great relief.

Dear Father Michael,

You ask for the text which most gives me assurance, but I don't really think there is one. My assurance – which is absolute – comes from Jesus himself: His living Presence. But there are the verses I most think of:

1 Corinthians, I, 30:

Christ Jesus "has become our wisdom, and our virtue and our holiness and our freedom".

2 Corinthians, I, 19-20.

"the Son of God, Christ Jesus ... was never yes and No: with Him it was always yes. However many the promises God made, the yes to them all is in Him:"

I'm sorry my handwriting is so unpleasing but I've tried my best:

affectionately Sister Wendy

HOUSE OF COMMONS
LONDON SW1A 0AA

17 May 2000

From Tony Benn

Dear Fr Michael,

Just a line to send the quotation below for **The Anthology of Assurance** which I hope will do.

LAO TZU ON LEADERSHIP

Go to the people
Live amongst them
Start with what they have
Build on what they know
And when the deed is done
The mission accomplished
Of the best leaders
The people will say
"We have done it ourselves"

Do feel free to use this in your auction.

Good luck with your fundraising.

With best wishes,

Telegraph Group Limited

CANADA SQUARE CANARY WHARF LONDON E14 5DT
DX42657 ISLE OF DOGS

FROM CONRAD BLACK
Chairman

30 May, 2000

Dear Father Seed.

An Anthology of Assurance

In response to your request, I think the words of Cardinal Newman's prologue to the Second Spring are ones which I find inspirational as well as comforting.

> *We have familiar experience of the order, the constancy, the perpetual renovation of the material world which surrounds us. Frail and transitory as is every part of it, restless and migratory as are its elements, never ceasing as are its changes, still it abides. It is bound together by a law of permanence, it is set up in unity; and, though it is ever dying, it is ever coming to life again. Dissolution does but give birth to fresh modes of organization, and one death is the parent of a thousand lives. Each hour, as it comes, is but a testimony, how fleeting, yet how secure, how certain, is the great whole. It is like an image on the waters, which is ever the same, though the waters ever flow. Change upon change, - yet one change cries out to another, like an alternative Seraphim, in praise and in glory of their Maker. The sun sinks to rise again; the day is swallowed up in gloom of the night, to be born out of it, as fresh as if it had never been quenched. Spring passes into summer, and through summer and autumn into winter, only the more surely, by its own ultimate return, to triumph over that grave, towards which it resolutely hastened from its first hour. We mourn over the blossoms of May, because they are to wither; but we know, withal, that May is one day to have its revenge upon November, by the revolution of that solemn circle which never stops, which teaches us in our height of hope, ever to be sober, and in our depth of desolation, never to despair.*

I hope you judge this suitable. and send you every good wish.

Yours. Conrad Black

REGISTERED IN ENGLAND No. 451593 RECYCLED PAPER

1O DOWNING STREET
LONDON SW1A 2AA

THE PRIME MINISTER

Dear Michael,

Many thanks for your letter.

My most inspiring and encouraging text is from St Mark's Gospel, Chapter IV. It is the passage where Christ calms the storm:

4:36	And when they had sent away the multitude, they took him even as he was in the ship. And there were also with him other little ships.
4:37	And there arose a great storm of wind, and the waves beat into the ship, so that it was now full.
4:38	And he was in the hinder part of the ship, asleep on a pillow: and they awake him, and say unto him, Master, carest thou not that we perish?
4:39	And he arose, and rebuked the wind, and said unto the sea, Peace, be still. And the wind ceased, and there was a great calm.
4:40	And he said unto them, Why are ye so fearful? how is it that ye have no faith?
4:41	And they feared exceedingly, and said one to another, What manner of man is this, that even the wind and the sea obey him?

I wish you every success with *An Anthology Of Assurance*.

yours true

Tony

Father Michael Seed

Southgate Road, London N1 3JP

24 · V · 2000

Dear Father Michael,

Yes, I am pleased to contribute to your Anthology of Assurance. Here is my contribution. I suspect that it may not have given me strength "in times of difficulty", but I have no doubt that it hugely inspired and encouraged me to be involved in the campaign for the abolition of capital punishment — the text is framed in my study, a gift from a famous Dutch criminologist, W H Nagel. The Sacco/Vanzetti case was almost the first case I read of an execution of two anarchists who received an egregiously unfair trial, because the judge was palpably biased and the prosecutor cheated. I also wondered about the jury's deliberations.

Yours sincerely,

Louis Blom-Cooper

If it had not been for these thing, I might have live out my life talking at street corners to scorning men. I might have die, unmarked, un-known, a failure, now we are not a failure. This is our career and our triumph, never in our full life could we hope to do such work for tolerance, for joostice, for man's onderstanding of man as now we do by accident. Our works – our lives – our pains nothing! The taking of our lives – lives of a good shoemaker and a poor fish peddler – all! That last moment belongs to us – that agony is our triumph.

Statement composed by Nicola Sacco, a shoemaker, on behalf of himself and his co-accused, Bartolomeo Vanzetti, a fish peddlar, on the eve of their execution for murder, on 23 August 1927. They had been arrested in May 1920 for the hold-up and murder of a guard and payroll clerk. They were tried in Dedham, Massachusetts; they were convicted and sentenced to death.

MICHAEL BLAKEMORE

15 May 2000

Dear Father Michael,

Work is not the whole of life, but if you're lucky enough to care about what you do, it can comprise a very important part. My work is mainly in the theatre, an absorbing world but not one renowned for its modesty, patience or lack of hysteria.

The following words of Anton Chekhov, written to his actress wife, are the best advice I've ever read to someone trying to make their way in the Arts (or, come to think of it, in anything else). We should all learn them by heart.

> *"You must stop worrying about success or failure, your business is to work step by step, from day to day, softly-softly, to be prepared for unavoidable mistakes and failures, in a word, follow your own line and leave competition to others."*

With every good wish

Michael Blakemore

22/5/00

Dear Michael.

It is with pleasure I send you the following, written by
an unknown child in a Nazi death camp. (From "Forms of
Prayer, Days of Awe" p.807 RSGB)

"From tomorrow on I shall be sad
 From tomorrow on, not today.
 Today I will be glad and every day
 no matter how bitter it may be
I shall say
 From tomorrow on I shall be sad
 Not today."

God bless

Yours

Lionel Blue.

7th July 2000

Dear Michael

Not only does The Lord move in mysterious ways, but He's also on The Net..

As a result I've tracked down the hymn I was chasing which often runs through my head when things get tough.

I've also been searching for a reference for The darkest hour being before the Dawn, but it's only thrown up a bunch of websites of disturbing origin. But it's another image that comes to mind — usually in a tent at night with lions around, when you really do want to believe daylight isn't far away.

It's a metaphor, of course. But isn't everything these days?

Best wishes as ever

Yours

Rory.

Arthur Hugh Clough. 1819–1861

Say not the struggle naught availeth,
The labour and the wounds are vain,
The enemy faints not, nor faileth,
And as things have been they remain.

If hopes were dupes, fears may be liars;
It may be, in yon smoke conceal'd,
Your comrades chase e'en now the fliers,
And, but for you, possess the field.

For while the tired waves, vainly breaking,
Seem here no painful inch to gain
Far back, through creeks and inlets making,
Comes silent, flooding in, the main.

And not by eastern windows only,
When daylight comes, comes in the light;
In front the sun climbs slow, how slowly!
But westward, look, the land is bright!

1O DOWNING STREET
LONDON SW1A 2AA

From the Office of Cherie Booth QC   14 April 2000

Dear Father Michael.

You asked me to send you passage or text which has inspired or encouraged me or given me strength in times of difficulty.

I am always found the Magnificat a beautiful part of St. Lukes Gospel.
It is the words Mary spoke when visiting her kinswomen Elizabeth after she learnt she was pregnant.

"My soul magnifies the Lord,
and my spirit rejoices in God my Saviour,
for he has regarded the low estate of his handmaiden.
For behold, henceforth all generations will called me blessed;
for he who is mighty has done great things for me,
and holy is his name.

And his mercy is on those who fear him
from generation to generation.
He has shown strength with his arm,
he has scattered the proud in the vanity of their hearts,
he has put down the mighty from their thrones,
and exalted those of low degree;
he has filled the hungry with good things,
and the rich he has sent empty away.
He has helped his servant Israel,
in remembrance of his mercy,
as he spoke to our fathers,
to Abraham and to his children for ever."

Yours
Cherie

CHERIE BOOTH QC

Noel Botham

August 2000

Dear Father Michael,

In 1966 I wrote *A Fighting Chance*, the story of the incredible journey by John Ridgway and Chay Blyth, who rowed across the Atlantic in 92 days.

I was particularly drawn to Chay Blyth, who went on to become the most intrepid sea adventurer of the twentieth century. His beliefs were simple but immensely strong and his spirit unquenchable.

Two quotations he gave me became, and still are, of great inspiration to me in my own life.

He told me: "I hate death and have very little time for prophecies and ill omens. There are a million things I have not done yet that I am determined to have a go at before I die."

And he introduced me to his favourite quotation from Percy Shelley, which became my own.

To suffer woes which hope thinks infinite,
To forgive wrongs darker than death or night,
To defy power which seems omnipotent,
Never to change, nor falter, nor repent.
This is to be good, great and joyous, beautiful and free,
This alone, life, joy, empire and victory.

My very best regards

Noel Botham

Kingston-upon-Thames
12 th May, 2000

Dear Father Seed,

Thank you for inviting me to share
with you and others a text which
has inspired me and which has
given people strength in time of difficulty.
My niece, Guli (38), wife of Svet and
mother of Alexandra, Olivia and
Svet Anthony, herself suffering from
the severe effects of breast cancer,
composed this song as a birthday
present for one of her best friends.
In this song Guli, tried to captivate
her friends feelings for her daughter,
Anne, who was born severely
handicapped.
Guli died three weeks after she
sang this song and launched
her CD.
I wish you inspiration with your
Anthology of Assurance.
Yours Sincerely,

Nico L. Brenninkmeyer

Unconditional Love
A Song for Anne

"The Sound of Life"
Ingi and Friends
Melody: Jacques Brel

Unconditional love,
That's what our life is about
That's what you taught us
You as a child, not the other way around
Life for you is still full of joy despite
Your pain and constant fight
You still can smile
Look at me for a while
And you seem to say: Mum
We can't change life, this is who I am.

I do love you
With heart and soul I do love you
My source of energy and zest for life
So deeply I love you.

Sometimes sadness overwhelms me
That is a fact because inevitably
As a parent you try to shield your child
From so much anguish, so much pain.
But then the sun will shine again
Because you make us laugh and live
That's what you will so freely give
And what you teach us with your life.

I do love you
With heart and soul I do love you
My source of energy and zest for life
So deeply I do love you.

Your arrival in our lives
Gave us an obvious mandate
One that we want to cherish
And see as much more than fate
Oh, dear Anne, I love you to be
For ever very close to me
You are a blessing for us all
Your love your life is pivotal
I do love you
With heart and soul I do love you
My source of energy and zest for life
So deeply I love you.

Mr S Brenninkmeyer

Esher
Surrey

25/05/2000

Dear Father Michael

Many thanks for your letter regarding 'An Anthology of Assurance.' I think the new book is a wonderful idea and am delighted to be able to contribute. I have a copy of 'I Will See You in Heaven', and it has brought me a lot of comfort in difficult times.

The passage I am enclosing is from Angela Ashwin "The Book of a Thousand Prayers" and is very dear to my heart as my wife and I find a lot of strength in its prayers for us and our children.

I wish you all the very best with the book and if I can be of further help, please do not hesitate to contact me.

With best wishes

Stephen Brenninkmeyer

Enc.

Jesus, where are you taking me?
Into joy.
Into pain.
I am afraid, but to do anything other than go
with you would be to die inwardly;
and to look for wholeness apart from you
would be to lose my true self.
So I come to you, protesting and confused,
but loving you all the same.
You will have to hold on to me as we walk together
through this compelling and frightening landscape
of the kingdom of God.

J Sainsbury plc

Sir George Bull
Chairman

Stamford House
Stamford Street
London SE1 9LL

www.j-sainsbury.co.uk

03 May 2000

Dear Father Michael

Further to your letter of 26th April I am happy to give below the text of a passage that has always stood me in good stead as an example to be followed. It sets out the example that I have tried to follow over time but, I am sure, with many lapses.

The extract is taken from a small book entitled "The colours and customs of the Coldstream Guards" which was issued to junior officers on their joining the Regiment, in my case almost 50 years ago.

Yours Sincerely

George Bull

Registered office as above
Registered number 185647 England

The following words of advice are given to all young Officers of the Regiment:

(i)　Always remember that you are a Coldstreamer, and whether on or off duty, to do all you can to act up to the high standard of which the history of the Regiment gives evidence. Never do anything which falls below that standard.

(ii)　Always set a good example to those under you, and never expect them to do what you would not do yourself.

(iii) Always work with your men, and do not delegate to your juniors or to NCOs what you should do yourself. On no account, however, discourage initiative or a sense of responsibility. Get to know your NCOs and men, look after their interests, and make it your business to help them find employment when they leave the Army.

Dear Fr Michael

I have derived much consolation from the enclosed
poem by Father John O Donoghue. I hope it suffices
for your purposes.

If you believe, as I do, that a prayer for
someone is to a great extent the expression
of loving kindness, good wishes and
agreeable intent towards someone, then if it's
a prayer for a mother you want, you need go
no further than this. But I think with only
a tiny shift of emphasis it can be made to
apply to any loved one. It is the epitome
of a loving longing for only good things for
a beloved person .

Also, we regularly read the 91st psalm with
our daughters in mind whenever they are away
- it is our prayer for a safe return and for
their happiness.

With all good wishes

Gay Byrne

8/5/00

Beannacht: for Josie, my mother: John O Donoghue

On the day when the weight deadens on your shoulders
and you stumble,
may the clay dance to balance you.
And when your eyes freeze behind the gray window
and the ghost of loss gets into you,
may a flock of colours, indigo, red, green and azure blue
come to awaken in you a meadow of delight.

When the canvas frays in the currach of thought
and a stain of ocean blackens beneath you,
may there come across the waters a path of yellow moonlight
to bring you safely home.
May the nourishment of the earth be yours,
may the clarity of light be yours,
may the fluency of the ocean be yours.
may the protection of the ancestors be yours.

And so may a slow wind work these words of love around you,
an invisible cloak to mind your life.

Evening Standard

NORTHCLIFFE HOUSE, 2 DERRY STREET, KENSINGTON, LONDON W8 5EE. 020 7938 6000

Dear Michael,

I have selected the passage on joy and sorrow from The Prophet by Kahlil Gibran. I have always found his words most calming and encouraging in times of difficulty.

Yours,

Sholto.

Then a woman said, Speak to us of Joy and Sorrow.

And he answered:

Your joy is your sorrow unmasked.

And the selfsame well from which your laughter
rises was oftentimes filled with your tears.

And how else can it be?

The deeper that sorrow carves into your being, the
more joy you can contain.

Is not the cup that holds your wine the very cup that
was burned in the potter's oven?

And is not the lute that soothes your spirit the very
wood that was hollowed with knives?

When you are joyous, look deep into your heart and
you shall find it is only that which has given you
sorrow that is giving you joy.

When you are sorrowful, look again in your heart,
and you shall see that in truth you are weeping for
that which has been your delight.

Some of you say, 'Joy is greater than sorrow,' and
others say, 'Nay, sorrow is the greater.'

But I say unto you, they are inseparable.

Together they come, and when one sits alone with
you at your board remember that the other is asleep
upon your bed.

Verily you are suspended like scales between your
sorrow and your joy.

Only when you are empty are you at standstill and
balanced.

When the treasure-keeper lifts you to weigh his gold
and his silver, needs must your joy or your sorrow
rise or fall.

Rt Hon Lord Callaghan of Cardiff KG

25th May 2000

Dear Father Seed

Thank you for your telephone call, following my letter of 17th May, giving Lord Callaghan a renewed opportunity to make a contribution to the book you are collating for charitable purposes, and he would like to send you the following verse by William Blake from "The Age of Innocence" for inclusion.

> *"To see a World in a grain of sand,*
> *And a Heaven in a wild flower,*
> *Hold Infinity in the palm of your hand,*
> *And Eternity in an hour"*

I hope you will find this of some use to your project.

Yours sincerely

Gina Page
Private Secretary to Lord Callaghan

Lambeth Palace
London

Dear Father Michael,

It is in the context of anxieties, lack of hope and such fears about the future, both personal and universal, that we turn to look again at what the Christian faith affirms. The calm and assured message of the Bible does not disregard the realities of which these fears are the expression. But in facing them and interpreting them, it assures us that whatever the future holds, *God is*, and is as Bishop David Jenkins used to say 'as he is in Jesus'. The Christian hope does not depend on an almanac which gives us a date when Christ will return in victory; but it insists that we may rely on it. He *will* return. There *will be* an establishing in totality of his kingdom of love, light and justice, the mode of which can only be glimpsed in picture language. For beyond the Four Last Things – death so familiar and so unyielding, judgement so feared and rebelled against, hell expressing all that is ultimately most negative and destructive, and heaven, that dream of high delight in the immediate presence of God to be enjoyed for ever – beyond even these is the *Last Thing* of all, on which all depends: the immortal and eternal God.

> There, in that other world, what waits for me?
> What shall I find after that other birth?
> Not stormy, tossing, foaming sea,
> But a new earth.
> No sun to mark the changing of the days,
> No slow, soft falling of the alternate night,
> No moon, no star, no light upon my ways,
> Only the Light.
> No gray cathedral, wide and wondrous fair,
> That I may tread where all my fathers trod,
> Nay, nay, my soul, no house of God is there,
> But only God.

Mary Coleridge.

+ George Cantuar

George Carey,
Archbishop of Canterbury

Father Michael Seed s.a.   22 May 2000

Dear Michael,

Thank you for your letter. I am enclosing a passage from 'Holiness' by Donald Nicholl. I knew Donald and the passage is about the assurance given by Jesus to the good thief on the . Cross. It combines good theology and simplicity which I find both inspiring and encouraging.

Yours ever,

Denis

LORD CARTER

What does all this mean for those of us who have been even faintly touched, no matter how faintly, by the 'sadness of not being a saint'? For it has been made clear to us that the climax of the whole creation is self-sacrifice; that is the ultimate in reality; there is nothing beyond it; it is the end. There is the kingdom of heaven. At the same time it appears that the capacity for self-sacrifice which the saints display only develops in those who have become spontaneous, pure and innocent through joyfully embracing suffering. Most of us, on the other hand, are still very much beginners; we find ourselves neither spontaneous nor pure nor innocent and we shrink from suffering. We feel to be far from the end, from the ultimate, far from the kingdom of heaven.

And yet here, once again, we stumble across another of those paradoxes with which the spiritual quest is strewn. For if we ask ourselves who, of all the characters in the Gospels, was the one first to recognize the kingdom of heaven on Jesus' own terms, we come up with an unexpected answer. Certainly the professionally holy people, the Jewish scribes and Pharisees, did not recognize his kingdom; nor, clearly, did the Roman authorities and soldiers who in one way or another mocked Jesus' title of king. Nor were his own disciples any more perceptive; from all accounts they wanted their own kind of kingdom where they would be sitting in the judgement seats. Even the most faithful group of all, the women who followed Jesus, do not seem to have grasped what he was offering to them.

In fact there is only one person who is recorded in the Gospels as accepting the kingdom of heaven on Jesus' own terms, and he was, like Jesus, a condemned criminal nailed to a cross. As he hung there, in his last agony, it was the 'good thief' who proclaimed Jesus to be innocent when he said, 'Lord, remember me when thou comest into Thy kingdom'. The good thief had recognized that even though he himself did not possess that purity by means of which the holy ones can 'penetrate and pervade all beings', nevertheless the Holy One himself could penetrate and pervade all beings, including dying criminals such as himself – Jesus was able to come into the place of a good thief and cleanse it and make it spotless for the final consummation. This he did, and that instantly, being 'more mobile than all motion'; hence Jesus did not promise the good thief a place in the kingdom tomorrow, or at some future date, but 'today' – that is, now, instantly, without any preparation.

Without any preparation the good thief, that total beginner, arrived at the end in an instant. The moment he began he was at the end. So perhaps the whole of this book is at the end superfluous, since all anyone need do – so long as he does it with his whole heart – is to say, 'Lord, remember me when thou comest into Thy kingdom.' Because then he will hear words that will banish every sadness; he will even forget the sadness of not being a saint when he hears the reply from Jesus, 'Today thou shalt be with me in Paradise'.

From: **Dame Barbara Cartland, D.B.E. D.St.J.**

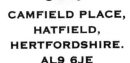

**CAMFIELD PLACE,
HATFIELD,
HERTFORDSHIRE.
AL9 6JE**

April 18 2000

Dear Father Michael,

Thank you so much for your letter.

I wrote the following lines many years
ago :-

The world was unknown, a mysterious place,
An adventure to move, to breathe in the sun.
To get to the top was only a race
Anyone could run.

That was youth, when everything was new,
Full of ideals and faith a vivid flame,
Unspoilt, untired and courageous too,
Living a game.

Slowly the idols fall, bitter to know,
That friends no longer friendly, envy, defame
Tired of the battle, getting old and slow
Until we rise again.

How little we appreciate our youth, how
profligate we are with the years as they fly
by. Only as we grow older do we cherish
every hour, every minute of each day because
the sands are running out.

With all my very best wishes for a
successful fund raising.

DAME BARBARA CARTLAND, D.B.E. D.St.J.

Edward Idris Cardinal Cassidy

22nd May 2000

Dear Father Michael,

At last, I have found a little time to reflect on your circular letter of April 17th last regarding the publication **AN ANTHOLOGY OF ASSURANCE** that you have been invited to edit. Fortunately, I am still well within the time limit indicated in your request.

The text that I have chosen is one that has been of particular assurance to me over the past ten years in my work as President of the Pontifical Council for Promoting Christian Unity and of the Holy See's Commission for Religious Relations with the Jews. When I have tended to frustration or despair because of the slow rate of progress or new challenges along the way, I have been reminded of the fact that our task is to "throw out the net", to do our best to co-operate with the Holy Spirit. On that we will be judged, not on the catch which the Lord will provide.

So when I need to be reassured in my ministry in time of disappointment and frustration, I turn to the Gospel of St. John 21:1-6 and read as follows:

> Later on, Jesus revealed himself again to the disciples. It was by the Sea of Tiberias, and it happened like this. Simon Peter, Thomas called the Twin, Nathanael from Cana in Galilee, the sons of Zebedee and two more of his disciples were together. Simon Peter said, 'I'm going fishing'. They replied, 'We'll come with you'. They went out and got into the boat, but caught nothing that night.
> When it was already light, there stood Jesus on the shore, though the disciples did not recognise that it was Jesus. Jesus called out, 'Haven't you caught anything, friends?' And when they answered, 'No', he said, 'Throw the net out to starboard and you'll find something'. So they threw the net out and could not haul it in because of the quantity of fish.

Certainly, the Lord continues to be full of surprises for those who are willing to listen to him and, at his command, to throw out the net.

Yours sincerely in the Risen Lord,

Edward Idris Cardinal Cassidy
President

THE BISHOP OF LONDON

Dear Michael,

Thank you for your letter about the "Anthology of Assurance". I like my assurance to be oblique and find it difficult to regard anything full frontal as really convincing. Like Dorothy Parker I prefer those dealing in assurance to "tell it to me slant".

One of the topics on which I find modern people needing a good deal of assurance is that of the dignity and significance of human life itself. There is a high rhetoric of human rights, which dominates the public stage but the sacred gift of life is being threatened at both ends of the earthly spectrum. Modern ways of looking at the world have reduced some people to the idea that human beings are little more than utensils for conveying genetic material, aimlessly, through the generations. Assurance in such circumstances does not come with a hearty slap on the shoulder and cheery generalities but with the conviction that comes from God through the poetic vision. The truth is that human life is less than human if it is not related to the divine. When this truth is spelled out, as it is in the poems of Thomas Traherne, then assurance is credible.

As ever,

Richard London:

Richard Chartres

The Salutation

These little Limmes,
These Eys and Hands which here I find,
These rosie Cheeks wherwith my Life begins,
Where have ye been,? Behind
What Curtain were ye from me hid so long!
Where was? in what Abyss, my Speaking Tongue?

When silent I,
So many thousand thousand yeers,
Beneath the Dust did in a Chaos lie,
How could I Smiles or Tears,
Or Lips or Hands or Eys or Ears perceiv?
Welcom ye Treasures which I now receiv.

I that so long
Was Nothing from Eternitie,
Did littIe think such Toys as Ear or Tongue,
To Celebrat or See:
Such Sounds to hear, such Hands to feel, such Feet,
Beneath the Skies, on such a Ground to meet.

New Burnisht Joys !
Which yellow Gold and Pearl excell!
Such Sacred Treasures are the Lims in Boys,
In which a Soul doth Dwell;
Their Organized Joynts, and Azure Veins
More Wealth include, then all the World contains.

From Dust I rise,
And out of Nothing now awake,
These Brighter Regions which salute mine Eys,
A Gift from GOD I take.
The Earth, the Seas, the Light, the Day, the Skies,
The Sun and Stars are mine; if those I prize.

Long time before
I in my Mother's Womb was born,
A GOD preparing did this Glorious Store,
The World for me adorne.
Into this Eden so Divine and fair,
So Wide and Bright, I com his Son and Heir.

A Stranger here
Strange Things doth meet, Strange Glories See;
Strange Treasures lodg'd in this fair World appear,
Strange all, and New to me.
But that they mine should be, who nothing was,
That Strangest is of all, yet brought to pass.

HILLARY RODHAM CLINTON

July 21, 2000

Dear Father Michael:

I am pleased to contribute to *An Anthology of Assurance* with a favorite passage of mine from Jesus' Sermon on the Mount. These words have encouraged me throughout my life.

"And seeing the multitudes, he went up into a mountain: and when he was set, his disciples came unto him:
And he opened his mouth, and taught them, saying,
'Blessed are the poor in spirit: for theirs is the kingdom of heaven.
'Blessed are they that mourn: for they shall be comforted.
'Blessed are the meek: for they shall inherit the earth.
'Blessed are they which do hunger and thirst after righteousness: for they shall be filled.
'Blessed are the merciful: for they shall obtain mercy.
'Blessed are the pure in heart: for they shall see God.

'Blessed are the peacemakers: for they shall be called the children of God.
'Blessed are they which are persecuted for righteousness' sake: for theirs is the kingdom of heaven.
'Blessed are ye, when men shall revile you, and persecute you, and shall say all manner of evil against you falsely, for my sake.
'Rejoice, and be exceeding glad: for great is your reward in heaven: for so persecuted they the prophets which were before you.'"

Matthew 5:1-12

With fellowship and appreciation for your good works, I am

Sincerely yours,

Hillary Rodham Clinton

Hillary Rodham Clinton

TERENCE CONRAN

5 June 2000

Dear Michael / Sued

I have chosen a wonderful passage written by Elizabeth David on Italian fish markets. Her beautiful style of writing has always greatly fascinated me, and I often refer to her work as a source of inspiration. Read this passage through, and by the end of it I can almost guarantee you will have the most incredible image of Venice in your mind.

Of all the spectacular food markets in Italy, the one near the Rialto in Venice must be the most remarkable. The light of a Venetian dawn in early summer – you must be about at four o'clock in the morning to see the market coming to life – is so limpid and so still that it makes every separate vegetable and fruit and fish luminous with a life of its own, with unnaturally heightened colours and clear stencilled outlines. Here the cabbages are cobalt blue, the beetroots deep rose, the lettuces clear pure green, sharp as glass. Bunches of gaudy gold marrow-flowers show off the elegance of pink and white marbled bean pods, primrose potatoes, green plums, green peas. The colours of the peaches, cherries and apricots, packed in boxes lined with sugar-bag blue paper matching the blue canvas trousers worn by the men unloading the gondolas, are reflected in the red-rose mullet and the orange *vongole* and *cannestrelle* which have been prised out of their shells and heaped into baskets. In other markets, on other shores, the unfamiliar fishes may be livid, mysterious, repellent, fascinating, and bright with splendid colour; only in Venice do they look good enough to eat. In Venice even ordinary sole and ugly great skate are striped with delicate lilac lights, the sardines shine like newly-minted silver coins, pink Venetian *scampi* are fat and fresh, infinitely enticing in the early dawn.

The gentle swaying of the laden gondolas, the movements of the market men as they unload, swinging the boxes and baskets ashore, the robust life and rattling noise contrasted with the fragile taffeta colours and the opal sky of Venice – the whole scene is out of some marvellous unheard-of ballet.

Hope this gets the gastric juices moving! Best wishes

Terence Conran

Terence Conran

23 May 2000

Dear Father Seed,

I have found comfort in the often quoted passage which follows, although the authorship is variously ascribed and the text appears in a variety of forms.

"We seem to give them back to Thee, O God, who gavest them to us. But as Thou didst not lose them in giving, so do we not lose them by their return. Not as the world giveth, givest Thou, O Lover of souls. What Thou givest Thou takest not away, for what is Thine is ours also if we are Thine. And life is eternal and love is immortal, and death is only a horizon, and a horizon is only the limit of our sight. Lift us up, strong Son of God, that we may see further; cleanse our eyes that we may see more clearly; draw us closer to Thyself that we may know ourselves to be nearer to our loved ones who are with Thee. And while Thou dost prepare a place for us, prepare us also for that happy place, that where they are and Thou art we may be also for evermore".

I hope that this may be suitable for your collection.

Yours sincerely

Clyde.

The Rt. Hon The Lord Clyde

From: Major General Sir Simon Cooper, KCVO

BUCKINGHAM PALACE

22nd May, 2000.

Dear Michael

One of my first recollections as a 13 year old schoolboy at Winchester was the funeral of the late Lord Wavell whose cortege, led by a sole piper playing the Flowers of the Forest, passed through lines of young Wykehamists to the 13th century cloisters. It made a great impression on me, and the life of that gallant soldier, leader and statesman, a man whose straightness of character and sensitivity was such an example to those who served him, became an inspiration and beacon to me as I passed through my own small military career.

Lord Wavell gathered together a number of poems, all of which I believe he could recite, into an anthology of verses entitled "Other Men's Flowers". I have kept a copy of that book all my life and while I have never been able to emulate his ability to remember each and every poem, they have been for me an assurance in life in many and varied circumstances when I have felt the need for strength, encouragement and respite from the pressures of day to day life.

The verses reach into mystery and the mystical, mark courage, love and sadness, show light heartedness and deeper thought and meet death with equanimity.

Lines which however are not included but stand out for me as for very many people as a single unbroken promise for the future are Minnie Louise Haskins:

"And I said to the man who stood at the gate of the year 'Give me a light that I may tread safely into the unknown'. And he replied 'Go out into the darkness and put your hand into the hand of God. That shall be to you better than a light and safer than a known way.' So I went forth and finding the hand of God, trod gladly into the night. And he led me towards the hills and the breaking of the day in the lone East."

Yours ever

Simon

Master of the Household

8th May 2000

Dearest Father Michael

How lovely to hear from you again. I loved meeting you and I hope to see you again soon,. What a lovely idea for an anthology, I enclose a copy of one of my very favourite poems by George Herbert, it is called The Flower and it shows that even after great loss and intense unhappiness the heart recovers and its owner is able to pick up the pieces.

Lots of love,

JILLY COOPER

Enc.

From: *The Flower*

Who would have thought my shrivelled heart
Could have recovered greenness? It was gone
    Quite under ground, as flowers depart
To feed their mother-root when they have blown;
    Where they together
    All the hard weather,
Dead to the world, keep house unknown.

These are thy wonders, Lord of Power,
Killing and quickening, bring down to hell
    And up to heaven in an hour;
Making a chiming of a passing-bell.
    We say amiss,
    This or that is:
Thy word is all, if we could spell.

. . . .

And now in age I bud again,
After so many deaths I live and write;
    I once more smell the dew and rain,
And relish versing: O my only light,
    It cannot be
    That I am he
On whom thy tempests fell all night.

8th May 2000

Dear Father Michael

I have chosen four reading: praise, thanks, a meditation and finally petition.

God our Father,
open our eyes to see your hand at work
in the splendour of creation,
in the beauty of human life.
Touched by your hand our world is holy.
Help us to cherish the gifts that surround us,
to share your blessings with our brothers and sisters,
and to experience the joy of life in your presence.
Through Christ our Lord.

I will praise you, Lord, you have rescued me
and have not let my enemies rejoice over me.

Lord, I cried to you for help
and you, my God, have healed me.
O Lord, you have raised my soul from the dead,
restored me to life from those who sink into the grave.

Sing psalms to the Lord, you who love him,
give thanks to his holy name.

His anger lasts but a moment; his favour through life.
At night there are tears, but joy comes with dawn.

I said to myself in my good fortune:
'Nothing will ever disturb me'.
Your favour had set me on a mountain fastness,
then you hid your face and I was put to confusion.

To you Lord, I cried,
to my God I made appeal:
'What profit would my death be, my going to the grave?
Can dust give you praise or proclaim your truth?'

The Lord Listened and had pity.
The Lord came to my help.
For me you have changed my mourning into dancing,
you removed my sackcloth and girdled me with joy.
So my soul sings psalms to you unceasingly.
Lord my God, I will thank you for ever.   Psalm 29.

Thee, God, I come from, to thee go,
All day long I like fountain flow
From the hand out, swayed about
Mote-like in thy mighty glow.

What I know of thee I bless,
As acknowledging thy stress
On my being and as seeing
Something of thy holiness.

Once I turned from thee and hid,
Bound on what thou hadst forbid;
Sow the wind I would; I sinned:
I repent of what I did.

Bad I am, but yet thy child.
Father, be thou reconciled,
Spare thou me, since I see
With thy might that thou art mild.

I have life before me still
And thy purpose to fulfil:
Yea a debt to pay thee yet:
Help me, sir and so I will.

But thou bidst, and just thou art,
Me shew mercy from my heart
Towards my brother, every other
Man my mate and counterpart.

Gerald Manley Hopkins

Lord, support us all the day long
until the shades lengthen and the evening comes,
and the busy world is hushed,
and the fever of life is over,
and our work is done.
Then, Lord, in your mercy,
grant us a safe lodging, and peace at last. Amen.

I do hope that these prayers and the poem will help others as much as they helped me in bad times + good

All the very best for a great success with the book.

Best good wishes
Anthea Craigmyle.

EUROPEAN PARLIAMENT

NIRJ JOSEPH DEVA DL FRSA MEP
MEMBER OF THE EUROPEAN PARLIAMENT

**For the South East of England
Spokesman for Overseas Development
and Co-operation**

1ˢᵗ June 2000

My dear Fr. Michael

PARADISE LOST

Thank you for inviting me to submit a passage of text that has inspired me in time of difficulty.

I remember losing my parliamentary seat in the general election of 1997. Though the indications were always against us, we fought to win all the way to polling day; but on May 2ⁿᵈ I was out of a job - as was my wife Indra who worked all the hours in the day as my secretary. No counselling, no redundancy - and just a few days before my 49ᵗʰ birthday, I had now to consider a complete career change.

So it was in these subdued circumstances I happened to be re-reading Paradise Lost, by Milton, and as I turned over the final page, I realised that the future lay ahead of me, with all the surprises and shocks it has always had in the past.

The extracts I have chosen are the closing lines of the poem. Eve and Adam are preparing to leave one life and embark upon another. The opening words are Eve's.

Chapter XII, lines 614-end

> *"... but now lead on;*
> *In mee is no delay; with thee to go,*
> *Is to stay here; without thee here to stay,*
> *Is to go hence unwilling; thou to mee*
> *Art all things under Heav'n, all places thou,*
> *Who for my wilful crime art banisht hence.*

This further consolation yet secure
I carry hence; though all by mee is lost,
Such favour I unworthy am vouchsaf't,
By mee the Promis'd Seed shall all restore."

      So spake our Mother Eve, and Adam heard
Well pleas'd, but answer'd not; for now too nigh
Th'Archangel stood, and from the other Hill
To their fixt Station, all in bright array
The cherubim descended; on the ground
Gliding Metéorous, as Ev'ning Mist
Ris'n from a River o'er the Marish glides,
And gathers ground fast at the Labourer's heel
Homeward returning. High in Front advanc't,
The brandisht Sword of God before them blaz'd
Fierce as a Comet; which with torrid heat,
And vapour as the Libyan air adust,
Began to parch that temperate Clime; whereat
In either hand the hast'ning Angel caught
Our ling'ring Parents, and to th'Eastern Gate
Led them direct, and down the Cliff as fast
To the subjected Plain; then disappear'd.

They looking back, all th'Eastern side beheld
Of Paradise, so late their happy seat,
Wav'd over by that flaming Brand, the Gate
With dreadful Faces throng'd and fiery Arms:
Some natural tears they dropp'd, but wip'd them soon;
The World was all before them, where to choose
Their place of rest, and Providence their guide:
They hand in hand with wand'ring steps and slow,
Through Eden took their solitary way.

With best wishes,

NIRJ DEVA

PROFESSOR BARRY FANTONI

May 22 2000

Dear Michael:

Although I have spent most of my life living in London I am an Italian. As I grow older, I dream more and more of living in Italy, in the land of my father. I would like to die there, where I feel my heart has its home. But as time goes by, the more I make plans, the harder it gets. I feel I am never going to make it and this thought fills me with a great sorrow. The city of Constantin Cavafy mirrors my feelings perfectly and this reflected, shared experience is a great comfort. There have been times when I have read The City daily.

Yours in God.

Barry Fantoni

The City

You said: "I'll go to another country, go to another shore,
find another city better than this one.
Whatever I try to do is fated to turn out wrong
and my heart—like something dead—lies buried.
How long can I let my mind moulder in this place?
Wherever I turn, wherever I look,
I see the black ruins of my life, here,
where I've spent so many years, wasted them, destroyed them totally."

You won't find a new country, won't find another shore.
This city will always pursue you.
You'll walk the same streets, grow old
in the same neighbourhoods, turn grey in these same houses.
You'll always end up in this city. Don't hope for things elsewhere:
there's no ship for you, there's no road.
Now that you've wasted your life here, in this small corner,
you've destroyed it everywhere in the world.

John Dewe Mathews,

1. 5. 2000

Dear Fr. Michael,

The following quotation from St Thomas Aquinas has always been of great inspiration to me.

"The mind should teach
the heart to feel;
the heart should teach
the mind to see".

Everytime I draw or paint, whether it be a human figure, animal or object or landscape I try to recollect on these words.

With love

Johnny DM.

17th April 2000

Dear Father Seed,

Many thanks for yours of April 12th concerning your new
anthology.

I feel that when it comes to passages of either prose or
poetry that have always caused me to slip into a contemplative
mood, there has never been anything to match Grey's Elegy
in a Country Churchyard.

There is a simple beauty about the way Grey uses language,
an evocation of the timelessness of the land and of the unknown
people who loved it and worked on it and who lie beneath
the stones in his local churchyard.

It is a passage I am never able to read without thinking
upon the futility of fame and fortune and the inevitability
of the coming eternity.   Simply reading these lines always
manages to put any foolish notions I may have about success
and wealth firmly back into perspective.

Sincere regards

Frederick Forsyth

19 April.

Dear Michael

Here is a favourite text. It is
by R S Thomas, the finest
poet of the last century.

Tony
[signature]

In Church

Often I try
To analyse the quality
Of its silences. Is this where God hides
From my searching? I have stopped to listen,
After the few people have gone,
To the air recomposing itself
For vigil. It has waited like this
Since the stones grouped themselves about it.
These are the hard ribs
Of a body that our prayers have failed
To animate. Shadows advance
From their corners to take possession
Of places the light held
For an hour. The bats resume
Their business. The uneasiness of the pews
Ceases. There is no other sound
In the darkness but the sound of a man
Breathing, testing his faith
On emptiness, nailing his questions
One by one to an untenanted cross.

SIR RONNIE FLANAGAN, OBE, MA
CHIEF CONSTABLE

BROOKLYN
KNOCK ROAD
BELFAST
NORTHERN IRELAND BT5 6LE

Our Ref: COM SEC 98/905/24

10 May 2000

Dear Dr. Michael,

Thank you for writing to let me know of your proposal to edit 'An Anthology of Assurance'.

I would, of course, be delighted to contribute to such a worthy project and have therefore enclosed a most thought-provoking poem from Robert Graves titled 'In Broken Images'. I trust this will be helpful.

With sincere best wishes.

Yours ever,

R FLANAGAN
Chief Constable

In Broken Images

He is quick, thinking in clear images;
I am slow, thinking in broken images.

He becomes dull, trusting to his clear images;
I become sharp, mistrusting my broken images.

Trusting his images, he assumes their relevance;
Mistrusting my images, I question their relevance.

Assuming their relevance, he assumes the fact;
Questioning their relevance, I question the fact.

When the fact fails him, he questions his senses;
When the fact fails me, I approve my senses.

He continues quick and dull in his clear images;
I continue slow and sharp in my broken images.

He in a new confusion of his understanding;
I in a new understanding of my confusion.

SIR GEORGE GARDINER

Dear Michael

There are two texts which gave me great assurance and strength in the darkest days of my political career at Westminster, when I found myself torn between what I saw as loyalty to my country's interests and supporting Prime Minister John Major in forcing the Maastricht Treaty though the Commons without any referendum, and subsequently insisting on a "wait and see" policy over whether we should scrap the pound and join the European Single Currency in the lifetime of the Parliament starting in 1997.

The first was a speech by Winston Churchill, some time after he survived the machinations of Tories in his Woodford constituency to de-select him because of his opposition to the appeasement of Adolph Hitler:

'The first duty of a Member of Parliament is to do what in his faithful and disinterested judgement he believes is right and necessary for the honour and safety of our beloved country. The second duty is to his constituents, of whom he is the representative but not the delegate. It is only in the third place that a man's duty to party organisation or programme takes rank. All three loyalties should be observed, but there is no doubt of the order in which they stand in any healthy manifestation of democracy.'

The second came from William Shakespeare (Hamlet, I.iii):

'This above all - to thine own self be true
And it must follow, as the night the day,
Thou canst not then be false to any man.'

With sincere good wishes,

George Gardiner

The Salvation Army

International Headquarters

101 QUEEN VICTORIA STREET
LONDON EC4P 4EP

OFFICE OF
THE GENERAL

28 April 2000

Dear Father,

Thank you for inviting me to make a contribution to your *Anthology of Assurance*. It won't surprise you to note that the text which has always brought me the most comfort is that which is found in 1 Corinthians 1:27a (KJV):

God hath chosen the foolish things of the world to confound the wise.

It has always been a matter of amazement to me that the Almighty seems to be ready to rely on very imperfect people in the achieving of His purpose. It is enormously comforting to discover the word 'chosen' in the passage which suggests that God has expressly decided to use the limited, the damaged, and the maimed as instruments in His hand for miraculous and often very beautiful projects.

Most servants of the Lord are conscious of their imperfections and often wonder, as I certainly do, why He does not look around for better people, nobler people, more capable people than myself. But as Paul clearly reminds us, the power of God is more clearly revealed when it is demonstrated and expressed in inadequate instruments.

Thank you for allowing me to comment, and I hope the above is of use to you.

Most sincerely yours,

JOHN GOWANS

WILLIAM BOOTH
Founder

JOHN GOWANS
General

ΟΙΚΟΥΜΕΝΙΚΟΝ
ΠΑΤΡΙΑΡΧΕΙΟΝ

ECUMENICAL
PATRIARCHATE

ΙΕΡΑ ΑΡΧΙΕΠΙΣΚΟΠΗ ΘΥΑΤΕΙΡΩΝ ΚΑΙ ΜΕΓΑΛΗΣ ΒΡΕΤΑΝΙΑΣ
ARCHDIOCESE OF THYATEIRA AND GREAT BRITAIN

30th May 2000

Dear father Michael,

Christ is Risen!

Thank you for your letter of 26th April in which you ask me to contribute the passage or text that has most inspired or encouraged me and given me strength in time of difficulty to a book entitled "*An Anthology of Assurance*" that you have been invited to edit.

As you will appreciate, in the long years of my life there have been many passages that have given me inspiration at different times and in different places.

However, something that comes to mind, and which to me are special, are these verses taken from the Office of the Little Canon of Supplication to the Most Holy Mother of God (which I use in Greek, but of which I give an English translation):

By many temptations I am held fast,
and seeking salvation
come for refuge in flight to you,
O Mother of God's own Word and Virgin,
from my dread dangers and troubles now rescue me.

As protection I set you and as a shield of my life,
you gave birth to God, Virgin Mother, guide me as a pilot now
into your anchorage,
you the support of the faithful,
source of all good things, you alone the one all-praised.

All those, loving Virgin, you protect,
with your mighty hand, who in faith come
to seek refuge with you;
for we sinners, bowed beneath the weight of many faults,
have no other who in our dangers and our afflictions
is ever-present intercessor before God,
Mother of God, the Most High,
whence we fall before you, 'Deliver
all your servants in every predicament'.

Joy of all who are afflicted,
champion of all dealt injustice,
the food of those who are in need,

you, the stranger's advocate, support and staff of the blind,
loving care of the sick are you, to all who are crushed down
shield, defence and aid are you, the orphan's succour and help,
Mother of our God the Most High,
hasten, All-Immaculate, hasten,
hear our prayer, deliver all your servants.

    In addition, I take great comfort from the following, which are taken from the service for Pentecost.

Heavenly King, Paraclete, Spirit of truth,
present everywhere, filling all things,
Treasury of blessings and Giver of life, come and dwell in us,
cleanse us from every stain,
and, O Good One, save our souls.

In your courts, Lord,
bending the knee of soul and body,
we the Faithful praise you,
the Father without beginning,
and the Son, likewise without beginning,
and the co-eternal and all-holy Spirit
who enlightens and sanctifies our souls.

    I also get great inspiration in difficult times from the prayer attributed to St. Ioannicius:

The Father is my hope,
the Son my refuge,
the Holy Spirit my protection.
Holy Trinity, glory to you.

               With best wishes and Paschal blessings

Gregorios
Archbishop of Thyateira
and Great Britain

General Sir Charles Guthrie GCB LVO OBE ADC Gen

Ministry of Defence
Main Building
Whitehall
London SW1A 2HB
United Kingdom

The Chief of the Defence Staff

D/CDS/15/12

8 May 2000

Dear Father Michael.

AN ANTHOLOGY OF ASSURANCE

My contribution is a soldier's prayer. It was used by Sir Jacob Astley (1579 – 1652) who was a Royalist Major General in the Civil War. He became a professional soldier at the age of 19 and served with distinction on the continent.

There is an eyewitness account that at the Battle of Edgehill (1642) Sir Jacob "before the charge made a most excellent, pious, short and soldierly prayer: for he lifted up his eyes and hands to heaven, saying 'O Lord! Thou knowst how busy I must be this day: if I forget Thee, do not Thou forget me.'"

I have used this prayer in many parts of the world and in many situations. It is brief but encourages and inspires and is appropriate for the hectic times we all find ourselves living in.

Yours Sincerely

Charles Guthrie

INVESTOR IN PEOPLE

HOUSE OF COMMONS
LONDON SW1A 0AA

LEADER OF THE OPPOSITION

WH/TM/se
21 June 2000

Dear Father Michael,

On my regular walks on the Yorkshire Dales, I am constantly struck by the beauty and vastness of the created world. I can fully identify with A M Toplady who apparently wrote this magnificent hymn, Rock of Ages, after seeking refuge in an outcrop of rock on a wet, wintry day:

ROCK OF AGES, cleft for me,
Let me hide myself in thee;
Let the water and the blood,
From thy riven side which flowed
Be of sin the double cure;
Cleanse me from its guilt and power.

Not the labours of my hands
Can fulfil thy law's demands;
Could my zeal no respite know,
Could my tears forever flow,
All for sin could not atone;
Thou must save, and thou alone.

The second verse of the hymn speaks powerfully of the limits of human endeavours when set against the grace of God. In all of life's uncertainties we can be confident in the Rock of Ages, which has outlasted and will outlast all nations and empires.

The Rt Hon William Hague MP

Father Michael Seed sa
Franciscan Friars

Alison Halford AM,
Delyn Constituency Office,
Greenfield Business Centre,
GREENFIELD,
Flintshire,
CH8 7QB.

Cynulliad Cenedlaethol Cymru
The National Assembly for Wales

Alison Halford AM

Wednesday, 24 May 2000

Ref: AhfrMSanth2452k

Dear *Fr. Michael,*

Thank you for your letter of 7th April, and my apologies for the delayed reply. I have been giving thought to what I would choose for your Anthology of Assurance. I toyed with this and pondered over that. In the end I have plumped for a poem that has been with me for many years, "The Hound of Heaven" by Francis Thompson.

This poem is full of significance for me: the thought that God is there when you turn to Him even if you have spent your life escaping Him is of immense reassurance for us all. "Rise, clasp My hand, and come!" and again ""I am He Whom thou seekest!" I know this poem has featured in many anthologies and that it is among the top 100 favourite poems in Britain. Perhaps I could have made a more original choice, but would prefer to be obvious than risk this lovely poem not being in your anthology.

Page size is difficult, as it will naturally depend upon your chosen format. If "Hound of Heaven" is too long, may I offer you a second choice from the beautiful works of Gerard Manley Hopkins, "The Lantern Out of Doors." Like so many of his poems this is infused with a reassuring certainty: "Christ minds," what more assurance can there be? May I offer you every success in this venture and that the completed anthology will bring a little light and comfort to those who buy it and for those whose benefit this is done. God bless your intentions.

Yours faithfully,

Alison Halford AM

The Lantern out of Doors

Sometimes a lantern moves along the night,
That interests our eyes. and who goes there?
I think; where from and bound, I wonder, where,
With, all down darkness wide, his wading light?

Men go by me whom either beauty bright
In mould or mind or what not else makes rare:
They rain against our much-thick and marsh air
Rich beams, till death or distance buys them quite.

Death or distance soon consumes them: wind
What most I may eye after? be in at the end
I cannot, and out of sight is out of mind.

Christ minds: Christ's interest, what to avow or amend
There, éyes them, heart wánts, care haúnts, foot fóllows kínd,
Their ránsom, théir rescue, ánd first, fást, last friénd.

31 May 2000

Dear Michael

Thank you for your letter of 15 May. I am delighted to contribute to "An Anthology of Assurance" and hope it will be successful in raising large sums for the two worthy causes which you have selected.

I hardly dare speculate on how much this letter itself may raise. I am not aware that any letter of mine has yet been sold. However, the bow-tie which I wore when Christine and I appeared on "Have I Got News For You" did raise £250 for charity by being exported to Russia!

I fear that the text which has most inspired me whilst I have patiently undergone my Job-like peregrinations in the last five years is, although perfectly pertinent, rather obvious: Kipling's "If".

> "If you can keep your head when all about you
> Are losing theirs and blaming it on you.
> If you can trust yourself when all men doubt you,
> But make allowance for their doubting too;
> If you can wait and not be tired by waiting,
> Or being lied about, don't deal in lies,
> Or, being hated, don't give way to hating,
> And yet don't look too good, nor talk too wise:
>
> If you can dream - and not make dreams your master;
> If you can think and not make thoughts your aim;
> If you can meet Triumph and Disaster
> And treat those two impostors just the same.
>
> If you can make one heap of all your winnings
> And risk it on one turn of pitch-and-toss,
> And lose, and start again at your beginnings
> And never breathe a word about your loss.
>
> If you can talk with crowds and keep your virtue
> Or walk with Kings - nor lose the common touch,
> If neither foes not loving friends can hurt you,
> If all men count with you, but none too much;

- 2 -

> If you can fill the unforgiving minute
> With sixty seconds' worth of distance run,
> Yours is the Earth and everything that's in it,
> And - which is more - you'll be a man, my son!"

It is this spirit which made it possible for me to resurface after having been submerged for the third time. If someone else has got this poem in before me, I would opt for Psalm 27 - which encouraged me when it came up at Matins at the start of my libel trial last autumn.

With best wishes
Yours ever
Neil

NEIL HAMILTON

GEORGINA HAMMICK

Father Michael Seed, s.a.

June 3rd, 2000.

Dear Father Michael

I'm sorry I'm late with the attached, and thank you for being so kind about it when we spoke on the telephone.

As you will see – and as I think I mentioned – I've chosen two passages which, in their very different ways, I find inspiring, encouraging and comforting. The psalm is perhaps nearer to your theme of assurance, but I leave you to choose.

It's an honour to be asked to contribute to the anthology – and thereby to the work of The Passage and of the Franciscan Friars of Atonement. Thank you for asking me.

Yours sincerely

Georgina Hammick

Spring

Nothing is so beautiful as Spring —
  When weeds, in wheels, shoot long and lovely and lush;
  Thrush's eggs look little low heavens, and thrush
Through the echoing timber does so rinse and wring
The ear, it strikes like lightnings to hear him sing;
  The glassy peartree leaves and blooms, they brush
  The descending blue; that blue is all in a rush
With richness; the racing lambs too have fair their fling.

What is all this juice and all this joy?
  A strain of the earth's sweet being in the beginning
In Eden garden. — Have, get, before it cloy,

  Before it cloud, Christ, lord, and sour with sinning,
Innocent mind and Mayday in girl and boy,
  Most, O maid's child, thy choice and worthy the winning.

Gerard Manley Hopkins

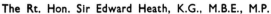

The Rt. Hon. Sir Edward Heath, K.G., M.B.E., M.P.

HOUSE OF COMMONS

15th July 2000

Dear Father Seed

Thank you for your letter.

I am glad that you like the text. It is one of my favourites.

With best wishes,

Yours sincerely

Edward Heath

Nicolas Breton
1545–1626

A worthy Merchant is the Heir of Adventure, whose hopes
hang much upon the Winds.

Upon a Wooden horse he rides through the World and in a
Merry gale makes a path through the seas.

He is a discoverer of countries and a finder-out of commodities,
resolute in his attempts and royal in his Expenses.

He is the life of traffic and the Maintenance of trade, the Sailors'
Master and the Soldiers' friend.

He is the Exercise of the Exchange, the honour of Credit, the
observation of time, and the understanding of thrift.

His Study is Number, his care his accounts, his Comfort his
conscience, and his Wealth his good name.

He fears not Scylla and sails close by Charybdis, and having
beaten out a Storm rides at rest in a harbour.

By his sea gain he makes his land purchase, and by the
Knowledge of trade finds the Key of his treasure.

Out of his travels he makes his discourses, and from his
Eye-observations brings the Model of Architecture.

He plants the Earth with foreign fruits, and knows at home
what is good abroad.

He is Neat in apparel, modest in demeanour, dainty in diet, and
Civil in his Carriage.

In sum, he is the pillar of a city, the enricher of a Country, the
furnisher of a Court, and the Worthy Servant of a King.

Lord Harris of High Cross

Father Michael Seed

30th May 2000

Dear Father Michael

Much as I would feel honoured to be included in your **Anthology of Assurance**, the choice of a favourite text poses a real corker of a question! Asked year or two ago, I would have promptly offered C S Lewis's poignant *A Grief Observed*, or taken time to search for an appropriate extract from Ronald Knox's luminous translation of *The Imitation of Christ*.

But since receiving your letter, my dear sister Violet - the last of my three siblings - departed this life aged 82 after a mercifully brief encounter with cancer. Her husband had died six months earlier following a long decline, through which she had nursed him with truly inspiring devotion. She plainly felt her wifely duties fully discharged and death retained for her no terror. But at my regular weekly visits, she frequently reverted to the loss of their only son Chris who, after a chequered youth including brushes with the law, emerged as a promising entrepreneur only to be struck down 10 years ago with a brain tumour in his mid-40s.

What were Christians to make of such apparently senseless, blind, "undeserved" adversity? After one such discussion, she handed me a piece of lined paper on which she had laboriously written out a poem by Ella Wheeler Wilcox. It had obviously given her comfort and consolation, and she asked me to type out copies for her grand-children. A few months later, one of them recited it at her funeral. How she would share my delight if her choice should now strike a chord with even a single grieving reader of this anthology!

Belief

The pain we have to suffer seems so broad,
set side by side with this life's narrow span
We need no greater evidence that God
hath some devine destiny for man.

So small this world, so vast its agonies,
a fuller life is needed to adjust
these ill-proportioned, wide discrepancies
between the spirit and its frame of dust.

A God would not allow this life to send
such crushing sorrows as pursue us here,
unless beyond this fleeting journey's end
our chastened spirits found a better sphere.

So when my soul writhes in some aching brief
and all my heart strings tremble at the strain,
my reason lends new courage to belief
and hidden purposes at last seem plain.

In the expectation that other contributors will produce further assurances, I look forward impatiently to publication. Since the proceeds are for charity, I hereby order a dozen copies, though as a professional economist (retired) I shall (still) look for a modest bulk discount!

With thanks for your initiative and every good wish for its abundant fulfilment.

Yours sincerely,
Ralph Harris

PS Pray omit this letter if you get enough better contributions - and cut my order to 6!.

Macmillan General Books

25 Eccleston Place
London
SW1W 9NF

www.panmacmillan.com

Dear Fr Michael,

Once again you've caught me at a bad time (workwise!), hence the delay.

However, I submit an old Chinese proverb that's always seemed right for me:

'_Rather light a candle than complain about the darkness._'

Hope you are well and _good_!

Yours sincerely
(and in sin!)

James Herbert

A Division of Macmillan Publishers Ltd

Registered Office:
Brunel Road, Houndmills,
Basingstoke, Hampshire RG21 6XS
Registered Number: 785998 England

Gopichand P. Hinduja

16 May 2000

Dear Father Seed,

Thank you for your letter dated 17 April requesting a passage that has inspired me the most. I have selected a set of verses from the Bhagavad-gita, a timeless scripture that is the essence of India's Vedic wisdom. It comes to us as a dialogue between the Supreme Personality of Godhead Sri Krishna, and His devotee Arjuna, whom he instructs on the science of self-realisation.

You may have heard that Henry David Thoreau wrote that in relation to the Gita, 'our modern world and its literature seem puny and trivial.' In my personal life, the Bhagavad-gita holds an answer to every situation I face – in business, social life, family life and on the path of devotion. It fills my heart with solace and joy that enlightens and uplifts my consciousness to higher realms of existence.

The following set of verses in which God describes the qualities that one must cultivate are resplendent with meaning and instruction. Once cultivated, these qualities will bestow on us the inner strength and inspiration that is required for peace and love.

adveṣṭā sarva-bhūtānāṁ maitraḥ karuṇa eva ca
nirmamo nirahaṅkaraḥ sama-duḥkha-sukhaḥ kṣamī

santuṣṭāḥ satataṁ yogī yatātmā dṛḍha-niścayaḥ
mayy arpita-mano buddhir yo mad-bhaktaḥ sa me priyaḥ

yasmānnodvijate loko lokān nodivjate ca yaḥ
harṣāmarṣa-bhayodvegair mukto yaḥ sa ca me priyaḥ

anapekṣaḥ śucir dakṣa udāsīno gata-vyathaḥ
sarvārambha-parityāgi yo mad-bhaktaḥ yo me priyaḥ

yo na hṛṣyati na dceṣṭi na śocati na kāṅkṣati
śubhāśubha-parityāgi bhaktimān yaḥ sa me priyaḥ

samaḥ śatrau ca mitre ca tathā mānāpamānayoḥ
śitoṣṇa-sukha-duḥkheṣu samaḥ saṅga-vivarjitaḥ

For UK correspondence
New Zealand House, 14th Floor, 80 Haymarket, London SW1Y 4TE

tulya-nindā-stutir maunī santuṣṭo yena kenacit
aniketaḥ sthira-matir bhaktimān me priyo naraḥ

ye tu dharmāmṛtam idaṁ yathoktaṁ paryupāsate
śraddadhānā mat-paramā bhaktās te 'tiva me priyāḥ

The Supreme Personality of Godhead said:
"One who is not envious but a kind friend to all living entities, does not think himself the proprietor and is free from false ego, equal in both happiness and distress, tolerant, always satisfied, self-controlled, and engaged in devotional service with determination, with mind and intelligence fixed on Me – such a devotee is very dear to Me.

He for whom no one is put into difficulty and who is not disturbed by anyone, who is equipoised in happiness and distress, fear and anxiety, is very dear to Me.

My devotee who is not dependent on the ordinary course of activities, is pure, expert, without cares, free from all pains, and not striving for fruitive results is very dear to Me.

One who rejoices nor grieves, who neither laments nor desires, and who renounces both auspicious and inauspicious things – such a devotee is very dear to Me.

One who is equal to friends and enemies, who is equipoised in honour and dishonour, heat and cold, happiness and distress, fame and infamy, always free from contaminating association, silent and satisfied with anything, doesn't care for any residence, is fixed in knowledge and engaged in devotional service – such a person is very dear to Me.

Those who follow this imperishable path of devotional service and who completely engage themselves with faith, making Me the supreme goal, are very very dear to Me."

I shall conclude with words of Mohandas K Gandhi, the Father of the Indian nation, "When doubts haunt me, when disappointments stare me in the face, and I see not one ray of hope on the horizon, I turn to the Bhagavad-gita and find a verse to comfort me and I immediately begin to smile in the midst of overwhelming sorrow. Those who meditate on the Gita will derive fresh joy and meanings from it every day."

Yours sincerely,

Gopichand P Hinduja
President, Hinduja Group of Companies

45/46 Poland Street, London W1V 4AU
Website: www.theoldie.co.uk

11. May 00

Dear Fr. Michael
Here is my comforting passage
for your collection -

Two Chinamen, behind them a third,
Are carved in lapis lazuli,
Over them flies a long-legged bird,
A symbol of longevity,
The third, doubtless a serving man,
Carries a musical instrument

Every discoloration of the stone,
Every accidental crack or dent,
Seems a water-course or an
                                    avalanche,
Or lofty slope where it still snows,
Though doubtless plum or cherry branch
Sweetens the little half-way house
Those Chinamen climb towards, and I
Delight to imagine them seated there
There, on the mountain and the sky,
On all the tragic scene they
                                    stare

OLDIE PUBLICATIONS LIMITED Registered in England and Wales. 2649845
Registered office address Lynton House. 7-12 Tavistock Square, London WC1H 9LT

One asks for mournful melodies;
Accomplished fingers begin to play.
Their eyes mid many wrinkles, their eyes,
Their ancient, glittering eyes, are gay.

from Lapis Lazuli
by W B Yeats

Hope you can read
my writing - Please say
a prayer for me
Regards

From Canon Eric James, DD, FKC

12. iv. 2000

Dear Fr. Michael,

Many thanks for your letter.

I am clear what has been the writing which has most inspired and encouraged me in times of difficulty. It's the poem "Love" of George Herbert:

LOVE bade me welcome; yet my soul drew back,
        Guilty of dust and sin.
But quick-eyed Love, observing me grow slack
        From my first entrance in,
Drew nearer to me, sweetly questioning,
        If I lacked anything.

'A guest', I answered, 'worthy to be here.'
        Love said, 'You shall be he.'
'I, the unkind, ungrateful? Ah, my dear,
        I cannot look on thee.'
Love took my hand, and smiling did reply,
        'Who made the eyes but I?'

'Truth, Lord, but I have marred them; let my shame
        Go where it doth deserve.'
'And know you not', says Love, 'who bore the blame?'
        'My dear, then I will serve.'
'You must sit down', says Love, 'and taste my meat.'
        So I did sit and eat.

Good wishes,

Yours ever

Eric

House of Lords · Westminster
01-219 3100

16ᵗʰ May 2000

Dear Michael,

Many years ago I first heard these words as grace before dinner. Since then they have been tucked into the blotter on my desk to bring a sense of assurance and comfort, and to put the trials and tribulations of the everyday world into proportion.

'May the road rise to meet you,
May the wind be always at your back,
May the sun shine warm on your face,
The rain fall softly on your fields,
And until we meet again,
May God hold you in the palm of his hand'

Yours Ever, Edward Jones

KENSINGTON PALACE

22nd May 2000

Dear Father Seed,

Thank you very much for your letter of 28th April and your request for an inspirational passage to be included in *An Anthology of Assurance* which will benefit the two charities, The Passage and the Franciscan Friars of the Atonement.

One of the most important lessons in life is surely learning how to deal with adversity. I cannot think of a greater reverse in worldly fortunes than that suffered by Queen Marie Antoinette of France and I have always been moved by the fortitude and dignity of the letter she wrote to her sister-in-law, Madame Elizabeth on the eve of her execution in 1793.

I wish you every success with the book and I look forward to its publication.

Yours sincerely

Her Royal Highness Princess Michael of Kent

Father Michael Seed, s.a.

October 16th, at half past four in the morning

"It is to you, Sister, that I am writing for the last time. I have just been sentenced to death, but not to a shameful one, since this death is shameful only to criminals, whereas I am going to rejoin your brother. Innocent like him, I hope to show the firmness which he showed during his last moments. I am calm, as one may well be when one's conscience is clear, though deeply grieved at having to forsake my poor children. You know that I existed only for them and for you, my good and affectionate sister. You who, in the kindness of your heart, had sacrificed everything in order to be with us – in what a terrible position do I leave you! It was only during the trial that I learned my daughter had been separated from you. Alas, poor child, I do not dare write to her, for she would not receive my letter; I do not even know if this one will reach you. However, through you I send them both my blessing, in the hope that some day, when they are older, they will be with you once more and will be able to enjoy your tender care. If only they will both continue to think the thoughts with which I have never ceased to inspire them, namely that sound principles and the exact performance of duties are the prime foundation of life, and that mutual love and confidence will bring them happiness. I trust my daughter will feel that at the age she has now reached she must always help her brother with the advice which her greater experience and her affection will enable her to give him; and that my son, in his turn, will give his sister all the care and will do her all the services which affection can stimulate; that they will both of them feel, whatever position they may find themselves in, they cannot be truly happy unless united – that they will take example from us. In our misfortunes, how much consolation we have derived from our mutual affection! Again, in happy times, one's enjoyment is doubled when one can share it with a friend – and where can one find a more affectionate, a more intimate friend than in one's own family? I hope my son will never forget his father's last words which I here purposely repeat for him: Let him never try to avenge our death!

I have to speak to you of one matter which is extremely painful. I know how much my little boy must have made you suffer. Forgive him, my dear sister;

remember how young he is, and how easy it is to make a child say whatever one wants, to put words he does not understand into his mouth. I hope a day will come when he will grasp the full value of your kindnesses and of the affection you have shown both my children.

It remains to entrust you with my last thoughts. I should have liked to write them before the trial opened; but, apart from the fact that I was not allowed to write, things have moved so swiftly that I really have not had time.

I die in the Catholic, Apostolic, and Roman religion, in that of my fathers, that in which I was brought up, and which I have always professed. Having no hope of any spiritual consolation, not even knowing whether there are still priests of this religion in France, and feeling that should there be such I should expose them to great risks were they to visit me here, I sincerely ask God's forgiveness for all the faults I have committed since I was born. I trust that, in His goodness, He will hear my last prayers, as well as those which I have long been making that, in His pity and His goodness, He may receive my soul.

I ask the forgiveness of all those whom I have known, and, especially of you, my sister, for the sorrow which, unwittingly, I may have caused them. I forgive my enemies the evil they have done me. I here bid farewell to my aunts and to my brothers and sisters. I had friends. The thought of being separated from them forever and of their distresses is among my greatest regrets in dying. Let them know, at least, that down to the last they were in my mind.

Adieu, my good and affectionate sister. I trust that this letter will reach you. Continue to think of me. I send you my most heartfelt love, and also to my poor, dear children. How heartbreaking it is to leave them forever! Adieu, adieu. I must now devote myself entirely to my spiritual duties. Since all my actions are under restraint, it is possible that they will bring a priest to me. I declare, however, that I shall not say a word to him, and that I shall treat him as an absolute stranger".

NEIL KINNOCK
VICE-PRESIDENT DE LA COMMISSION EUROPEENNE

Brussels, *11 May 00*

Dear Fr. Seed,

Thank you for your letter of 13 April.

I was interested to learn that you have been invited to edit 'An Anthology of Assurance' and am pleased to provide you with the following quote from Benjamin Franklin, written in 1772, which has always had special meaning to me:

> **We must not in the Course of Publick Life expect *immediate* Approbation and *immediate* grateful Acknowledgment of our Services. But let us persevere thro' Abuse and even Injury. The internal Satisfaction of a good Conscience is always present, and Time will do us Justice in the Minds of the People, even of those at present the most prejudic'd against us.**

Wishing you every success with your important work and the auction of the letters and texts.

Regards,

Neil Kinnock

Neil Kinnock

PS Franklin's words are reproduced in the original.

Winfield House

Dear Father Michael:

You asked about inspiring or encouraging texts. To me, the 8th chapter of Romans is the most powerful of all — with its glorious close ...

"For I am convinced
that neither death nor life,
neither angels nor demons,
neither the present nor the future,
nor any powers,
neither height nor depth —
Nor anything else in all creation
will be able to separate us
from the love of god
which is in Christ Jesus
our Lord."

Romans 8: 37-38

I also love the Psalms. Some favorites ... Psalms 18, 27, 34, 37, 56, 62, 91, 139, 146 ----.

Winfield House

And Psalm 118 ... verses 6-9
follow ...

The Lord is with me,
I will not be afraid.
What can man do to me?
The Lord is with me;
He is my helper ....
It is better to take refuge
in the Lord
than to trust in man.
It is better to take refuge
in the Lord
than to trust in
princes.

Blessings to you!

Linda Lader

PHILIP LADER

We know that in everything God works for good with those who love Him, who are called according to His purpose.

Romans 8:28

At every moment you choose yourself. But do you choose your self? Body and soul contain a thousand possibilities out of which you can build many "I's." But in only one of them is there a congruence of the elector and the elected. Only one — which you will never find until you have excluded all those superficial and fleeting possibilities of being and doing with which you toy, out of curiosity or wonder or greed, and which hinder you from casting anchor in the experience of the mystery of life, and the consciousness of the talent entrusted to you which is your "I."

Dag Hammarskjöld, Markings

JOHN LE CARRÉ   Cornwall

To   16 : iv : '00
Father Michael Seed, s.a.

Dear Father Michael,

     Thanks for your
letter of 12th April. In tough
times I consult my wedding
ring. Inside it, my wife
Jane had the engraver inscribe
a line of John Donne:
'No winter shall abate the
Spring's encrease' [sic].

     All good wishes,

John le Carré

SHUGBOROUGH
STAFFORD

The Donkey

When fishes flew and forests walked
    And figs grew upon thorn,
Some moment when the moon was blood
    Then surely I was born.

With monstrous head and sickening cry
    And ears like errant wings,
The Devil's walking parody
    On all four-footed things.

The tattered outlaw of the earth,
    Of ancient crooked will;
Starve, scourge, deride me: I am dumb,
    I keep my secret still.

Fools! For I also had my hour;
    One far fierce hour and sweet:
There was a shout about my ears,
    And palms before my feet.   G.K. Chesterton 1874-1936

MAGNUS LINKLATER

31 May 2000

Dear Father Seed,

What an impossible request! You ask for "the passage or text from whatever source which has most inspired or encouraged you and given you strength in times of difficulty." Different books suit different times. Writers who helped when one was young, no longer mean the same thirty years later. Moods shift, time alters perceptions. The writer, however, with whom I have felt most constantly at home, to whom I have been bound most often, from youth through middle age, is Robert Louis Stevenson. I cannot think of an author whose instinct for narrative, for humanity, and for the written word, has survived down the years with such freshness and purity. I could pick up any of his books tomorrow and die happy if I were told that it was the last I would read. Ideally it would be *Weir of Hermiston*.

When my dear friend David Blundy, a brave journalist, was killed in the course of duty, covering a distant war in a far-off place, I reached for words of comfort from RLS, and discovered these in one of his essays on writers who had influenced him. I quoted it at David's memorial service. It still brings tears to the eyes and comfort to the spirit:

"This brings us ... to a very noble book -- the *Meditations* of Marcus Aurelius. The dispassionate gravity, the noble forgetfulness of self, the tenderness of others, that are there expressed and were practised on so great a scale in the life of its writer, make this book a book quite by itself. No one can read it and not be moved. Yet it scarcely or rarely appeals to the feelings -- those very mobile, those not very trusty parts of man. Its address lies further back: its lesson comes more deeply home; when you have read, you carry away with you a memory of the man itself; it is as though you had touched a loyal hand, looked into brave eyes, and made a noble friend; there is another bond on you thenceforward, binding you to life and the love of virtue."

I wouldn't have mined writing that.

Yours sincerely,

Magnus Linklater

Magnus Linklater

21. V. 00

Dear Michael,

If it is not too late, I should be honoured and thrilled to be included — it sounds such a lovely book.

I have got the most encouragement from a book called :

True Humanism by

Jacques MARITAIN.

I first read it when I was having difficulty in entering the Church, (which I longed to do) on scientific and

political grounds. I greatly symp-
athised with the Humanists and
utterly rejected General Franco.

Maritain was not only
a great scientist but also
Jewish and an ardent
Roman Catholic.

Even if I only understood
one word or one sentence
in ten, that one was worth
everything else put together.

He, Maritain, argued that Humanism was invaluable — but it had to be _true_ _humanism_, and that was found within Christianity.

All best wishes from us both,

Elizabeth

From: The Earl of Longford KG, PC

14th April 2000

The Rev Michael Seed
St Francis Friary
47 Francis Street
Westminster
London SW1P 1QR

My dear Michael

I suppose that the three quotations which have meant most to me from the Gospels are these:-

1. I was in prison and you came to me.
2. The Son of Man has come to seek and to save those who are lost.
3. (from the Cross) Father forgive them for they know not what they do.

Frank

Strachur House,
Argyll.

24.4.2000

Dear Father Michael,
Thank you for your letter
asking me to contribute, to
'an Anthology of assurance'.—
I am sending you three
prayers that have helped me,
and will be honoured if you
include any of them and
decide to auction one or other.
I am a great admirer of
Cardinal Hume's charity The Passage.
and only wish I was younger
and lived in London so that I
could help it more practically—

Wishing you great success
in what seems a splendid
idea —. Yours sincerely
Veronica Maclean

Prayer for a good Death

Seigneur, ayez pitié de moi,
et à l'heure de ma mort
reçevez mon âme étonnée,
dans le sein de votre miséricorde.

Lord, have pity on me,
and at the hour of my death
receive my astonished soul
into the heart of your divine mercy.

HOUSE OF COMMONS
LONDON SW1A 0AA

**FROM THE PRIVATE SECRETARY TO
THE RT. HON. JOHN MAJOR, CH MP**

23rd May 2000

Dear Father Norman-

On behalf of Mr Major, I am writing to acknowledge your letter asking if he would submit a copy of a favourite text or verse which has given him strength or encouragement in the past.

Mr Major is glad to contribute to your book and I enclose a copy of *If* by Rudyard Kipling, which has been duly signed by Mr Major, as you requested.

With all good wishes,

Yours ever,

Arabella..

MISS ARABELLA WARBURTON

Father Michael Seed

IF

IF you can keep your head when all about you
Are losing theirs and blaming it on you;
If you can trust yourself when all men doubt you,
But make allowance for their doubting too;
If you can wait and not be tired by waiting,
Or being lied about, don't deal in lies,
Or being hated, don't give way to hating,
And yet don't look too good, nor talk too wise:

IF you can dream - and not make dreams your master;
If you can think - and not make thoughts your aim;
If you can meet with Triumph and Disaster
And treat those two impostors just the same;
If you can bear to hear the truth you've spoken
Twisted by knaves to make a trap for fools,
Or watch the things you gave your life to broken,
And stoop and build 'em up with worn-out tools:

IF you can make one heap of all your winnings
And risk it on one turn of pitch-and-toss,
And lose, and start again at your beginnings
And never breathe a word about your loss;
If you can force your heart and nerve and sinew
To serve your turn long after they are gone,
And so hold on when there is nothing in you
Except the Will which says to them 'Hold on!'

If you can talk with crowds - and keep your virtue,
Or walk with Kings - nor lose the common touch,
If neither foes nor loving friends can hurt you,
If all men count with you, but none too much
If you can fill the unforgiving minute
With sixty seconds' worth of distance run,
Yours is the Earth and everything that's in it,
And - which is more -
YOU'LL BE A MAN, MY SON!

Rudyard Kipling

19th May 2000

Dear Father Michael Seed.

It was kind of you to ask me to contribute to the work you are to about to edit but I am unable to quote any great text as my inspiration in good times, or my rock in times of distress. Two things, my belief in God and the advice given to me by my parents have provided these.

Without this belief in a power greater than man, a power that created everything we know, and then gave us the chance to grow in stature within this creation, I would have found coping with life and my eventual death impossible.

I would also have found coping with life difficult without the wisdom of my parents. I haven't always managed to live up to the standard they expected but at least their sound advice has stopped me making too much of a fool of myself.

Rule 1: Don't take yourself too seriously, always be prepared to laugh at yourself before you laugh at others.

Rule 2: Remember that you word is your bond, once given it's as binding as any contract.

Rule 3: Choose your wife with care and remember marriage only succeeds if you work at it, betray your wife and you betray yourself.

Rule 4: Never judge anyone by their colour, religion or anything other than the way they behave towards you and others.

Yours Sincerely
Terry Major-Ball.

Text chosen for the service of thanksgiving for Lord Menuhin:

Isaiah 55: 6 – end

Seek the Lord while he may be found, call upon
him while he is near. Let the wicked abandon their
ways, and the unrighteous their thoughts. Turn
back to the Lord, who will have mercy; to our
God, who will richly pardon us. For my thoughts
are not your thoughts, neither are your ways my
ways, says the Lord. As the heavens are higher than
the earth, so are my ways higher than your ways,
and my thoughts than your thoughts. As the rain
and the snow come down from heaven, and return
not again but water the earth, bringing forth life
and giving growth; seed for sowing and bread to
eat; so is my word that goes out from my mouth; it
will not return to me empty, but it will accomplish
my purpose; and succeed in the task I gave it.

18 May 2000

Dear Father Michael,

I have never really thought about this before but, as I muddle my way through life, I find I have been helped and guided by two strands of philosophy. The first was summed up by my late husband, Nicholas, who wrote:

> Whenever you propose to do anything, you should stop and ask yourself--'If everyone did this, what would the world be like?' You will soon discover the right answer.

As, with age, we increasingly have to come to terms with the loss of our dearest relatives and friends, it is a piece of Jewish wisdom that sustains me:

> Say not in grief that he is no more,
> But in thankfulness that he was.

With all good wishes,

Ann Monsarrat.

Ann Monsarrat

16 April 2000

From an early age I have always been fascinated by mountains, inspired originally by Mallory's comment "that it is there" when asked why he wanted to climb Everest. When I was at school, I took up rock climbing, mainly in North Wales or the Lake District, which I continued through University until I went to work overseas when other responsibilities took over. This respect and love for mountains was deeply embedded, and has always remained with me, so I take every opportunity to renew the experience.

The text that goes with this feeling is the 1st verse of Psalm 121 " I will lift up mine eyes unto the hills from whence cometh my help". Moses communed with God on Mount Sinai, Elijah tested the faithlessness of Ahab on Mount Carmel, and Jesus delivered his most significant preaching from the hills around Galilee. So there is nothing new about finding inspiration from mountains. Likewise I have found that sitting alone on or near mountain tops and gazing at surrounding peaks has helped me to think clearly, and make some of the most important decisions of my life, with an assurance that these are God given.

Viscount Montgomery of Alamein

23 May

Dear Father Michael Seed
Two quotations & something. Life should never
be taken too seriously

"When one subtracts from life infancy (which is vegetation) – sleep, eating and swilling – buttoning and unbuttoning – how much remains of downright existence? The summer of a dormouse."

BYRON JOURNALS

"They say the seeds of what we will do are in all of us, but it always seemed to me that in those who make jokes in life the seeds are covered with better soil and with a higher grade of manure."

ERNEST HEMINGWAY A MOVEABLE FEAST

ARCHBISHOP'S HOUSE,
WESTMINSTER, LONDON, SW1P 1QJ

29 June, 2000

Dear Michael,

I would like to give the following words for your anthology of assurance. These words are taken from the Mass and are said by the priest. They have always given me great assurance in my years as a priest.

"Lord Jesus Christ, you said to your apostles: I leave you peace, my peace I give you. Look not on our sins, but on the faith of your Church, and grant us the peace and unity of your kingdom where you live forever and ever. Amen."

Yours devotedly in Christ,

+Cormac Murphy-O'Connor

Archbishop of Westminster

St James's Palace
London

Dear Father Michael,

You wrote and asked me what passage or text has most encouraged and given me strength in times of difficulty. So far as the Scriptures are concerned - for me personally, and I suspect for many others - the words of the 23rd Psalm have always been immensely comforting and reassuring.

I have also never forgotten the former Speaker of the House of Commons - who later became Lord Tonypandy - telling me that when they were young they were so poor that their mother could not afford to buy them shoes. Understandably they were sometimes envious of other children - who seemed to be better off than they were. That was until one day - when he met a boy whose foot had been amputated as the result of an accident. "Never again," said George "did I allow myself to indulge in self pity."

When one gets down and depressed for whatever reason - it is well worth remembering that without exception there is always somebody who is worse off than oneself.

With kind regards -
Yours sincerely
Angus Ogilvy.

From - The Rt Hon Sir Angus Ogilvy KCVO

THE TIMES

Press Gallery, HOUSE OF COMMONS
Westminster, LONDON SW1A 0AA

12th April 2000

Dear Father Michael,

Thank you for your letter of the 7th April asking me for something from literature that has been a source of pleasure to me. I think the poem *I Remember, I Remember*, by Thomas Hood, is one of my favourite pieces and I quote it below.

1.   I remember, I remember
The house where I was born,
The little window where the sun
Came peeping in at morn;
He never came a wink too soon,
Nor brought too long a day,
But now, I often wish the night
Had borne by breath away!

2.   I remember, I remember
The roses, red and white,
The violets, and the lily-cups,
Those flowers made of light!
The lilacs where the robin built,
And where my brother set
The laburnum on his birthday, -
The tree is living yet.

3.   I remember, I remember,
Where I was used to swing,
And thought the air must rush as fresh
To swallows on the wing;
My spirit flew in feathers then,
That is so heavy now,
And summer pools could hardly cool
The fever on my brow.

4.   I remember, I remember,
The fir trees dark and high;
I used to think their slender tops
Were close against the sky:
It was a childish ignorance,
But now 'tis little joy
To know I'm farther off from heaven
Than when I was a boy.

I wish you well in your efforts to raise fund for your two charities and I am delighted to give you this little bit of help.

Yours sincerely,

Matthew Paris

Registered Office: Times Newspapers Limited, P.O. Box 495, Virginia Street, London E1 9XY
Registered No. 894646 England

The Rt. Hon. the Lord Owen CH

House of Lords,
Westminster,
London SW1A 0PW

16 May 2000

Dear Father Seed,

Thank you for your letter and I send my best wishes for your efforts in compiling An Anthology of Assurance which will be published by Continuum to raise funds for charity.

The text which is most evocative for me comes from St Paul's Epistle to the Ephesians. My grandfather, who was blind from the age of twelve, became a clergyman and was a very remarkable man. He was Vicar of Llandow and Lysworney in the Church of Wales. My mother, sister and I moved from Plymouth during the war and lived with my grandparents in Llandow. I remember attending the local school and in order to encourage me to improve my reading and to stand up in public my grandfather set a date when I would have to read the following passage from the Bible in his church. It was his favourite passage from the Bible and it has remained one of mine eversince and one which is identified in my own mind with my first minor achievement.

St Paul's Epistle to the Ephesians, Chapter 6, verses 10-20

> Finally, my brethren, be strong in the Lord, and in the power of his might.
> Put on the whole armour of God, that ye may be able to stand against the wiles of the devil.
> For we wrestle not against flesh and blood, but
> against principalities, against powers, against the rulers of the darkness of this world, against spiritual wickedness in high places.
> Wherefore take unto you the whole armour of God, that ye may be able to withstand in the evil day, and having done all, to stand.

The Rt. Hon. the Lord Owen CH

House of Lords,
Westminster,
London SW1A 0PW

Stand therefore, having your loins girt about with truth, and
having on the breastplate of righteousness;
And your feet shod with the preparation of the gospel of peace;
Above all, taking the shield of faith, wherewith ye shall be able to
quench all the fiery darts of the wicked.
And take the helmet of salvation, and the sword of the Spirit, which
is the word of God:
Praying always with all prayer and supplication in the Spirit, and
watching thereunto with all perseverance and supplication for all
saints;
And for me, that utterance may be given unto me, that I may open
my mouth boldly, to make known the mystery of the gospel.
For which I am an ambassador in bonds: that therein I may speak
boldly, as I ought to speak.

Yours sincerely

DAVID OWEN

THE RIGHT HONOURABLE

CHRISTOPHER PATTEN, CH

MEMBER OF THE EUROPEAN COMMISSION

17 May 2000

Dr Father Michael,

Thank you very much for your letter.

The passage which has regularly inspired me is the last paragraph of volume one of Karl Popper's "The Open Society and Its Enemies". It reads as follows:

"If we are tempted to rely on others and so be happy, if we shrink from the task of carrying our cross, the cross of humaneness, of reason, of responsibility, if we lose courage and flinch from the strain, then we must try to fortify ourselves with a clear understanding of the simple decision before us. We can return to the beasts. But if we wish to remain human, then there is only one way into the open society. We must go on into the unknown, the uncertain and insecure, using what means we may have to plan as well as we can for both security and freedom."

Best wishes.

May 4th 2000

Stobhall,
by Perth.

Dear Father Michael

At last I am answering your letter of April 13th.

It is hard to find the text you ask for "strength in Times of difficulty" Surely this calls for prayer — not I suspect what you seek!

What about " If you don't succeed at first, try, try again". I know this is a hackneyed phrase but for me it more or less meets your request but one must beware in case 'obstinacy' is the outcome!

Best regards

Sincerely David (Perth)

Lord Pilkington of Oxenford

Oxenford House
Ilminster
Somerset

House of Lords

29 April 2000

Dear Father,

I enclose a copy of a piece by Teilhard de Chardin. You may like to alter it or cut out various bits – I leave it entirely to you.

I hope that your book is a success.

Yours sincerely

The Lord Pilkington of Oxenford

Enc.

You know it Yourself Lord, through having borne the anguish of it as man: on certain days the world seems a terrifying thing: huge, blind and brutal. It buffets us about, drags us along, and kills us with complete indifference. Heroically, it may truly be said, man has contrived to create a more or less habitable zone of light and warmth in the midst of the great, cold, black waters – a zone where people have eyes to see, hands to help, and hearts to love. But how precarious that habitation is! At any moment the vast and horrible thing may break in through the cracks – the thing which we try hard to forget is always there, separated from us by a flimsy partition: fire, pestilence, storms, earthquakes, or the unleashing of dark moral forces – these callously sweep away in one moment what we had laboriously built up and beautified with all our intelligence and all our love.

Since my dignity as a man, O God, forbids me to close my eyes to this – like an animal or a child – that I may not succumb to the temptation to curse the universe and Him who made it, teach me to adore it by seeing You concealed within it. O Lord, repeat to me the great liberating words, the words which at once reveal and operate: *Hoc est Corpus meum*. In truth, the huge and dark thing, the phantom, the storm – if we want it to be so, is You! *Ego sum, nolite timere.* The things in our life which terrify us, the things that threw You Yourself into agony in the Garden, are, ultimately, only the Species or Appearance, the matter of one and the same Sacrament.

TIM PIGOTT-SMITH

April 20, 2000

Dear Father Michael

As a young actor, I found the disciplines of the theatre –the often unrewarding roles, the repetition – very hard to come to terms with. Then I remembered, and was often inspired by, a passage from J.D.Salinger's book <u>Franny and Zooey</u>…

Franny is an aspiring young actress. Her attitude to acting is in crisis. Zooey, her brother, talks to her on the phone, and reminds her of Seymour, their elder, now dead, brother, who created a fictitious "Fat Lady". Seymour's Fat Lady was someone for whom you did things – like polish your shoes when you were going to appear on the radio – if you didn't polish your shoes, no-one would see, but you were somehow letting the Fat Lady down! She is described as follows –

"…sitting on this porch all day, swatting flies, with her radio going full-blast from morning till night… with very – you know – very thick legs, very veiny… I figured the heat was terrible, and she probably had cancer and – I don't know what."

Zooey goes on…

"I don't care where an actor acts. It can be in summer stock, it can be over a radio, it can be over *tele*vision, it can be in a goddam Broadway theatre, complete with the most fashionable, most well-fed, most sunburned-looking audience you can imagine. But I'll tell you a terrible secret – Are you listening to me? *There isn't anyone out there who isn't Seymour's Fat Lady.* There isn't anyone *anywhere* that isn't Seymour's Fat Lady. Don't you know that? Don't you know that goddam secret yet? And don't you know – *listen* to me, now – *don't you know who that Fat Lady really is?* … Ah, buddy. Ah, buddy. It's Christ Himself. Christ Himself, buddy."

I love J.D Salinger, and I drew great reassurance from this passage, which I have cobbled together a bit – I hope he will forgive me – in mitigation, I think the Fat Lady would!.

Yours, with
very good wish

Tim Pigott Smith

Palais de Monaco

May 2, 2000

Dear Father

      Thank you for your kind letter of the 12th of April, 2000 and I am delighted to bring my personal contribution to your noble cause on behalf of people who are homeless.

      Please find hereunder the prayer which has most inspired and encouraged me whilst giving me strength in times of difficulty:

> O God, grant me the serenity to
> accept what I cannot change, the
> courage to change what I can, and
> the wisdom to know the difference.

      I wish you every success in your endeavours.

My prayers are with you,

Olga Polizzi, CBE

3/5/2000.

Dear Father Seed,

I write this in haste as
I am leaving for a ten day holiday –
I am very happy to give you a
text & will do so as soon as I get
back – I am afraid you will not
make much money auctioning my letter,
I will have to buy it myself!

Footprints

One night a man had a dream. He dreamed he was walking along the beach with the LORD. Across the sky flashed scenes from his life. For each scene, he noticed two sets of footprints in the sand: one belonging to him, and the other to the LORD.

When the last scene of his life flashed before him, he looked back at the footprints in the sand. He noticed that many times along the path of his life there was only one set of footprints. He also noticed that it happened at the very lowest and saddest times in his life.

This really bothered him and he questioned the Lord about it. "LORD, you said that once I decided to follow you, you'd walk with me all the way. But I have noticed that during the most troublesome times in my life. There's only one set of footprints. I don't understand why when I needed you most you would leave me."

The LORD replied, "My precious, precious child, I love you and I would never leave you. During your time of trial and suffering, when you see only one set of footprints, it was then that I carried you."

SIR CLIFF RICHARD

3 May 2000

Dear Michael

Thank you for your letter regarding 'An Anthology of Assurance'

I submit the following text:

Romans 8:28–29
For I am convinced that
neither death nor life,
neither angels nor demons,
neither the present nor the future,
nor any powers,
neither height nor depth,
nor anything else in all creation,
will be able to separate us from the love of God
that is in Christ Jesus our Lord.

With best wishes

Cliff Richard

Dear Fr. Michael,

The passage I have chosen that gives me assurance is from a novel by the Brazilian author Machado de Assis, first published in 1880, entitled *The Posthumous Memoirs of Braz Cubas.* The hero is thrown from the saddle of his donkey but one foot remains caught in the stirrup. He is saved by a muleteer. The hero is suitably grateful

> If the donkey had run away, I should have been really hurt, and who can say that death would not have been the outcome. A broken head, a congestion, an internal injury of some sort... The muleteer had perhaps saved my life; in fact I was sure of it; I felt it in my blood... I resolved to give him three of the five gold coins that I had with me; not because this was the value of my life – it would have been immeasurable – but because it was a reward worthy of the selflessness with which he had rescued me. Definitely I would give him three of the coins....
>
> I went though the saddlebags, took out an old waistcoat in the pocket of which I kept the five gold coins and, as I did so, wondered whether the reward was not excessive, whether two gold coins would not suffice. Perhaps one. In truth, one coin would be enough to give him shivers of joy. I looked at his clothes; he was a poor devil, who doubtless had never seen a gold coin. Therefore, one coin. I took it out, I saw it shine in the sunlight... I placed a silver crusade in his hand, mounted the donkey, and set off at a fast pace, a little troubled or, more precisely, a little uncertain about the effect of the silver coin. But at a short distance I looked back; the muleteer was bowing his thanks, and looked overjoyed. I thought that he must be so, indeed,; I had paid him well, perhaps too well. I put my fingers in the vest that I was wearing and felt some copper coins; they were pennies, which I should have given to the muleteer instead of the silver crusado. For, after all, he had not thought about a reward or about the virtue of his act, he had merely yielded to a natural impulse, to his temperament, to the habits of his trade. Furthermore, the fact that he had happened to be not father along the road nor father back but exactly at the point where the accident occurred seemed to indicate that he had been merely an instrument of Providence. One way or the other, there was really no personal merit in his act. This thought made me miserable; I called myself wasteful, I charged the crusado mentally to the account of my prodigal past. I felt (why not tell the whole truth?), I actually felt remorse.

Why does this passage give me assurance? Because it illustrates so well my own failings when it comes to charity and good works.

Piers Paul Read

THE LORD RIX Kt CBE DL

20.4.00

Dear Father Seed,

Thank you for your letter. I enclose an excerpt from my second autobiography. Farce About Face – which, in turn, included an excerpt from my first. You are free to print it, if you wish, with an acknowledgement.

It was because of Shelley and all the help I have received from fellow parents & Mencap over the years which drove me on.

Yours,

[signature]

She was born, after a forty-eight-hour labour, at 2.30 a.m. on Monday, December 3rd, in the Westminster Hospital. She was a funny little thing, like all newly born babies, but she seemed beautiful to us. We were in raptures. Elspet's father roared with laughter at us as she stuck her tongue out at him. She seemed to stick her tongue out rather a lot . . .

Elspet was a little worried. "They don't bring her to me as much as I'd like," she complained. "Do you think there's something wrong with her?"

"Don't be silly," I said, "all the babies seem to be kept away from their mums, except for feeding times."

But the early warnings had been sounded. Elspet remembered her strange feelings during pregnancy. Often she had thought the child she was carrying was not a normal child. She was, in the event, correct; but everyone was loath to tell us. It was the maternity sister, Sister Gilbert, who finally persuaded the gynaecologist, Mr Searle, to reveal the facts. "He'd like to see you in Harley Street at six o'clock tomorrow evening," she said in an off-hand way to me.

My reaction was understandably nervous. "What for? And why Harley Street? Why can't he see me here?"

She calmed me down: "It's just a routine interview he likes to have with all new fathers – away from the hurly-burly of the hospital."

So I reported this to Elspet and her fears multiplied, but I battened down my own feelings and attempted to encourage her. My fears, however, dragged side by side with hers and as I stepped into Mr Searle's consulting-room I had only to look at his face to know the worst.

It's laughable really. Actors perform these parts better than their actual counterparts. Mr Searle behaved like the newest drama student.

"Do come in . . . Do sit down . . . Do have a cigarette."

I came in, but I neither sat down nor had a cigarette. I was a non-sitter and a non-smoker in those situations. A non-smoker at all times, anyway.

"Have you heard of mongolism?" was his first question. Well that was one way of putting it. Direct and to the point. Our daughter was a mongol. My stomach went through his consulting-room floor and has never, really, recovered its rightful place since. "Have you heard of mongolism?" "I have to tell you your son has been killed in a car accident." "Your husband was a brave man." Jesus Christ! It's only in moments such as these that you realise the inadequacy of the spoken word. Afterwards you recognise that the poor devil stumbling and stuttering before you is as mortified and horrified at explaining the disaster as you are at receiving it. But that's the way we do it and what other way is there?

What indeed? I wrote those lines for my first autobiography, one cold, wet January midnight in 1974, huddled over my desk in my room at the Angel Hotel, Cardiff – weeping the while at the memory. My miserable stay in South Wales was occasioned by appearing in pantomime at the New Theatre, but we ran into Edward Heath's three-day week and the whole thing was a damp, unpleasant farrago. Perhaps that's what made my unhappiness all the greater, but the majority of parents are easily transported back to the shock of those first numbing words, when you learn your child is not as other children. Mongolism has now been dressed-up as Down's syndrome, of course, but the pain and grieving remain the same.

And so it was, when I first saw that advert in the *Guardian*, advertising the job of Secretary-General on Mencap, I only had to read it to Elspet – who was driving – for us both to realise that this was the way ahead for me. But first I had to get the job. It wasn't as easy to become the Secretary-General of MENCAP as I thought. And why did I want the job at that particular time, anyway? After all, Shelley had been around since 1951. I told you, it's a long story.

(from *Farce About Face*, published by
Hodder and Stoughton, 1989)

London SW18
http://www.tomrobinson.com

May 5, 2000

[handwritten: Dear Father Seed,]

The work which has most unfailingly given me support and comfort over the years has been T.S. Eliot's "Four Quartets" and perhaps the most moving single passage from those poems has been the following:

> When the train starts, and the passengers are settled
> To fruit, periodicals and business letters
> (And those who saw them off have left the platform)
> Their faces relax from grief into relief,
> To the sleepy rhythm of a hundred hours.
> Fare forward, travellers! Not escaping from the past
> Into different lives, or into any future;
> You are not the same people who left that station
> Or who will arrive at any terminus,
> While the narrowing rails slide together behind you;
> And on the deck of the drumming liner
> Watching the furrow that widens behind you,
> You shall not think "the past is finished!"
> Or "the future is before us."
>
> You are not those who saw the harbour
> Receding, or those who will disembark.
> Here between the hither and the farther shore
> While time is withdrawn, consider the future
> And the past with an equal mind.
>
> T.S. Eliot "The Dry Salvages"
> Section III, lines 9-22, 27-31

There isn't a single word or syllable out of place here; and you don't have to get the Bhagvad Gita reference in a line like "Fare forward travellers !"on first, second or even tenth reading. The beauty of the writing can be enjoyed for its own sake at any level you like. It never fails to move me.

I hope this will be of some help and interest for your anthology.

[handwritten: With all good wishes]

[signature]

Tom Robinson

17 April, 2000

My dear Michael

Thank you very much for your letter about *An Anthology of Assurance*.

I have sent out before the words of St Theresa which are fairly well known. If this is too familiar or I have sent it for something else like *Will I See You In Heaven?* please ask me again. However I am rather cumbered about with Holy Week at the moment and if this will suffice I am very happy you should do whatever you like with it. You have been so kind to me and I am afraid this is rather a poor return.

With best wishes.

Yours Ever

The Rt Revd Lord Runcie

Let nothing disturb thee,
Nothing affright thee;
All things are passing;
God never changeth;
Patient endurance
Attaineth to all things;
Who God possesseth
In nothing is wanting
Alone God sufficeth.

St. Teresa's Bookmark

29.5.00.

Dear Father Michael,

Thank you for your letter. The passage I would like to send you is from the book of Exodus, ch. 33 verses 17-23.

> And the Lord said unto Moses, I will do this thing also that thou hast spoken: for thou hast found grace in my sight, and I know thee by name.
>
> And he said, I beseech thee, shew me thy glory.
>
> And he said, I will make all my goodness pass before thee, and I will proclaim the name of the Lord before thee; and will be gracious to whom I will be gracious, and will shew mercy on whom I will shew mercy.
>
> And he said, Thou canst not see my face: for there shall no man see me, and live.
>
> And the Lord said, Behold, there is a place by me, and thou shalt stand upon a rock:
>
> And it shall come to pass, while my glory passeth by, that I will put thee in a clift of the rock, and I will cover thee with my hand while I pass by:
>
> And I will take away mine hand, and thou shalt see my back parts: but my face shall not be seen.

With best wishes for your project,

Yours sincerely,
Paddy Rossmore

ב״ה

OFFICE OF
THE CHIEF RABBI

Dear Father Michael,

The following passage, from the Book of Psalms, has been a source of strength to me at many difficult times. I dedicate it to the memory of the late Cardinal Hume, a true man of faith, who often told me that the Book of Psalms was central to his own spirituality:

> O God, You have examined me and You know:
> You know me in my sitting down and in my standing up;
> You have understood my thoughts from afar;
> You watch my road and my rest;
> You are familiar with all my paths.
> Before any word is on my tongue,
> O God, You know it.
> You surround me, You are in front and behind,
> And Your hand touches me.
> This understanding is marvellous and too much for me,
> It is high and I cannot grasp it.
> Where shall I go from your spirit?
> And where shall I hide from Your face?
> If I go up into the heavens You are there,
> And if I lie down among the dead You are there,
> If I take the wings of dawn and live in the furthest regions of the sea,
> Even there Your hand will guide me and Your right hand will hold me.
> (Psalm 139: 1-10)

Wishing you every success in your work,

Jonathan Sacks

Chief Rabbi Professor Jonathan Sacks

A DECADE OF JEWISH RENEWAL

חדש ימינו כקדם

In haste

Herewith a "mantra" I made up to sing (mentally) when the going got tough in a Marathon — in time with my footsteps.

Ive got food so everything OK
Ive got food so everything OK
Ive got food so its a lovely day
Yes
Ive got food so everything OK

Odd — but it works!

Sir Jim Savile

Roger Scruton,

Date: 17th April 2000

Dear Father Seed,

In times of real difficulty there is no solace, I find, better than
contemplating the death of Christ, as recounted in the gospels, and as set
to music by Bach. When distressed by hostility and injustice, I turn to
Valéry's *Le cimetière marin*, and to the famous lines

> *midi le juste y compose des feux*
> *La mer, la mer, toujours recommencée...*

Somehow the setting of this poem, the language, and the oblique
references to a civilisation which stretches before and after and which
justifies both suffering and piety, makes all the contest of the world fall
away, and death itself redemptive.

Yours sincerely,

Roger Scruton

FROM
PAUL SCOFIELD   21.ⅠⅤ.2000.

Dear Father Michael Seed.

Thank you so much for your letters, please accept my apologies for my late response, I have been away from home for a short while.

It is kind of you to ask me to contribute to "An Anthology of Assurance" and happily enclose a quote from St. Thomas More's writings, which was a source of strength to me when in New York for a year, playing Sir Thomas in the play "A Man For All Seasons". I cannot claim that I underwent hardship during that time, but confess that I longed to be at home with my family.

I hope the passage will serve your purpose.

Yours sincerely
Paul Scofield.

It is most kind of you to address me as Sir Paul, but I can only lay claim to the title of Mr. I mention this only so that you may not later discover an inaccuracy in your proofs.

P.S.

Give me thy grace, good Lord, to set the world at nought.
To set my mind fast upon thee.
And not to hang on the blast of men's mouths;
To be content to be solitary;
Not to long for wordly company;
Little and little to cast off the world
And rid my mind of the business thereof.
Not to long to hear of any worldly things.
Gladly to be thinking of God,
To lean unto the comfort of God.

Sir Thomas More,
written in the margin of his prayerbook.

Dear Father Michael Seed,

Thank you for your letter. I send you the passage from the Book of Common Prayer which always seems to sum up all the requests for reassurance which I fail to make.

ALMIGHTY God, the fountain of all wisdom, who knowest our necessities before we ask and our ignorance in asking: We beseech thee to have compassion upon our infirmities; and those things, which for our blindness we cannot ask, vouchsafe to give us for the worthiness of thy Son Jesus Christ our Lord. Amen.

Not much can slip through that net.

Sincerely Ned Sherrin

Tuscany   19° Apl. 200

Dear Fr Seed,

    In reply to your
letter I send you the following
text which I have always
held as a spiritual and
philosophical truth, vital
to the course of my life:

Ecclesiastes (Revised Version) 9, 11:

    I returned, and saw
under the sun, that the
race is not to the swift,
nor the battle to the strong,
neither yet bread to the wise,
nor yet riches to men of
understanding, nor yet favour
to men of skill; but time
and chance happeneth to
them all.

    With kind regards
     Yours sincerely
     Muriel Spark

ALTHORP

8th May, 2000.

Dear Father Michael,

I have thought further about your book, and would like to submit 'Into Battle', by Julian Grenfell, the War Poet, as my entry, please.

It is a beautiful work, rich in imagery: despair is there, but hope is certainly the victor.

I hope it is suitable for your anthology.

Yours sincerely,

Earl Spencer

Into Battle

THE naked earth is warm with spring,
    And with green grass and bursting trees
Leans to the sun's gaze glorying,
    And quivers in the sunny breeze;
And life is colour and warmth and light,
    And a striving evermore for these;
And he is dead who will not fight;
    And who dies fighting has increase.

The fighting man shall from the sun
    Take warmth, and life from the
      glowing earth;
Speed with the light-foot winds to run,
    And with the trees to newer birth;
And find, when fighting shall be done,
    Great rest, and fullness after dearth.

All the bright company of Heaven
    Hold him in their high comradeship,
The Dog-Star, and the Sisters Seven,
    Orion's Belt and sworded hip.

The woodland trees that stand together,
    They stand to him each one a friend;
They gently speak in the windy weather;
    They guide to valley and ridge's end.

The kestrel hovering by day,
    And the little owls that call by night,
Bid him be swift and keen as they,
    As keen of ear, as swift of sight.

The blackbird sings to him, 'Brother,
    brother,
    If this be the last song you shall sing,
Sing well, for you may not sing another;
    Brother, sing.'

In dreary, doubtfill, waiting hours,
    Before the brazen frenzy starts,
The horses show him nobler powers;
    O patient eyes, courageous hearts!

And when the burning moment breaks,
    And all things else are out of mind,
And only joy of battle takes
    Him by the throat, and makes him
    blind,

Through joy and blindness he shall know,
    Not caring much to know, that still
Nor lead nor steel shall reach him, so
    That it be not the Destin'd Will.

The thundering line of battle stands,
    And in the air Death moans and sings:
But Day shall clasp him with strong hands,
    And Night shall fold him in soft wings.

Sir Sigmund Sternberg
Sternberg Centre for Judaism, 80 East End Road, London N3

The Beautiful Interview

I had a dream I had an interview with God. " Come in," God said to me, " So, you would like to interview Me?" " If you have the time," I said.

God smiled and said " My time is called eternity and there is enough to do everything; what questions do you have in mind to ask me?"

" What's the one thing that surprises you most about mankind?"

God answered, " That they get bored of being children, are in a rush to grow up, and then long to be children again. That they lose their health to make money and then lose their money to restore their health. That by thinking anxiously about the future, they forget the present, such that they live neither for the present nor for the future. That they live as if they will never die, and they die as if they have never lived..."

God's hands took mine and we were silent.

After a long period, I said, " May I ask you another question? As a Parent, what would you ask your children to do?"

God replied with a smile: " To learn that they cannot make anyone love them. What they can do is to let themselves be loved. To learn that it takes years to build trust, and a few seconds to destroy it. To learn that what is most valuable is not what they have in their lives, but whom they have in their lives. To learn that it is not good to compare themselves to others. There will always be others better or worse than they are. To learn that a rich person is not one who has the most, but one who has the least. To learn that they should control their attitudes, otherwise their attitudes will control them. To learn that it only takes a few seconds to open profound wounds in persons we love, and that it takes as many years to heal them. To learn that there are persons that love them dearly, but simply do not know how to show their feelings. To learn that money can buy everything but happiness. To learn that while at times they may be entitled to be upset, that does not give them the right to upset those around them. To learn that they are masters of what they keep to themselves and slaves of what they say. To learn that they shall reap what they plant; if they plant gossip they will harvest intrigues, if they plant love they will harvest happiness. To learn that true happiness is not to achieve their goals but to learn to be satisfied with what they already achieved, or die from envy and jealousy of what they lack. To learn that two people can look at the same thing and see something totally different. To learn that those who are honest with themselves without considering the consequences go far in life. To learn that by trying to hold on to loved ones, they very quickly push them away; and by letting go of those they love, they will be side by side forever. To learn that even through the word "love" has many different meanings, it loses value when it is overstated.

Author Unknown

With my warmest personal regards,

Yours,

Sir Sigmund Sternberg

Sir John Stevens QPM
Commissioner of Police of the Metropolis

METROPOLITAN POLICE SERVICE

New Scotland Yard
Broadway
London SW1H 0BG

16 May 2000

Dear Father Seed

Thank you for your letter of 26 April to the Commissioner regarding a contribution to 'An Anthology of Assurance'.

The Commissioner has asked me to pass to you a piece of text which has had direct relevance to his policing career and family life over many years. The text is from Matthew 7 v.24-26 and although quite short is tremendously meaningful when building one's life upon principles, morals, integrity and family values.

The text is like a guiding principle which can be applied to many facets of life and the way it is conducted. It is simple but powerful and pivots around the need for strong foundations.

> *The Wise and Foolish Builders*
> 'Therefore everyone who hears these words of mine and puts them into practice is like a wise man who built his house on the rock. The rain came down, the streams rose, and the winds blew and beat against that house, yet it did not fall, because it had its foundation on the rock. But everyone who hears these words of mine and does not put them into practice is like a foolish man who built his house on sand. The rain came down, the streams rose, and the winds blew and beat against that house, and it fell with a great crash.'

Yours sincerely

Simon Humphrey
Chief Superintendent
Staff Officer to the Commissioner

THE TIMES

1 Pennington Street, London E1 9XN

From the Editor

For An Anthology of Assurance

To set in order, that's the task
Both Eros and Apollo ask;
For Art and Life agree in this,
That each intends a synthesis,
That order which must be the end
That all self-loving things intend
Who struggle for their liberty
Who use, that is, their will to be.

From New Year Letter 1941
By W. H. Auden   (56-63)

April 2000

Registered Office: Times Newspapers Limited, P.O. Box 495, Virginia Street, London E1 9XY
Registered No. 894646 England

British Broadcasting Corporation White City 201 Wood Lane London W12 7TS Telephone 0181 752 7500 Fax 0181 752 7599

B B C News

From Correspondent

Dear Michael,

How flattering to be asked to contribute to your anthology. My only hesitation about offering the piece below is that there must be a good chance that others will choose it too.

During my time at Cambridge I made the pilgrimage to Little Gidding with a group of fellow Eliot fans in a battered Datsun. It was an appropriately cold East Anglian winter's day, and we spent some innocent hours trying to work out which hedges would be "White again, in May, with voluptuary sweetness" and whether you could still find the "dull façade" if you "leave the rough road/And turn behind the pig-sty". I reread the Four Quartets for all sorts of reasons – including assurance. This is still my favourite passage.

> If you came this way,
> Taking any route, starting from anywhere,
> At any time or at any season,
> It would always be the same: you would have to put off
> Sense and notion. You are not here to verify,
> Instruct yourself, or inform curiosity
> Or carry report. You are here to kneel
> Where prayer has been valid. And prayer is more
> Than an order of words, the conscious occupation
> Of the praying mind, or the sound of the voice praying.
> And what the dead had no speech for, when living,
> They can tell you, being dead: the communication
> Of the dead is tongued with fire beyond the language of the living.
> Here, the intersection of the timeless moment
> Is England and nowhere. Never and always.

With kind regards,

Edward Stourton

May 1st, 2000

Dear Father Michael,
I have sung the following
lines many times in performances
of Handel's "Messiah" and they have
given me a great sense of comfort
and assurance.

"Come unto him all ye that labour, that are heavy
laden, and he will give you rest. Take his yoke
upon you, and learn of him, for he is meek and
lowly of heart, and ye shall find rest unto your
souls".

Matthew XI, 28-29

With best wishes

Joan Sutherland
OM, AC, DBE

Kiri Te Kanawa

16th May 2000

Dear Father Michael,

One of my favourite writers is Emily Dickinson. I dip into her poetry and prose time and time again and find it both reassuring and inspirational.

Following is a passage from The Diary of Emily Dickinson – by Jamie Fuller.

Wednesday, August 14

Thievery is afoot in the garden! Birds have beset the cherry trees – and carried off a large part of the treasure we assigned to pies. They do no more than Nature's bidding – but still one wishes for a scruple in their kingdom.

We shape nature with a garden. But if she don't approve the plan, she sends her flocks and earthy armies to alter it. She promises neither success nor failure – for all is one to her – and she is heedless of our efforts. It is we who put ourselves at her center – and praise ourselves for a perfect fruit. This summer, as in others, she has been kind to my flowers – which return my affection. Surrounded by such beauty we forget the hidden savagery. Nature gives – but may at any time withdraw.

With best wishes,

John M. Templeton

May 23, 2000

Dear Father Michael:

Thank you for your letter of April 26, which arrived May 23.

It is wonderful to hear you are helping these two charities. I am enclosing a copy of a poem by Rudyard Kipling called "If", which has been quite an inspiration to me during my 87 years.

God bless you,

John M. Templeton

Enclosure

IF you can keep your head when all about you
Are losing theirs and blaming it on you;
If you can trust yourself when all men doubt you,
But make allowance for their doubting too;
If you can wait and not be tired by waiting,
Or being lied about, don't deal in lies,
Or being hated, don't give way to hating,
And yet don't look too good, nor talk too wise:

IF you can dream – and not make dreams your master;
If you can think – and not make thoughts your aim;
If you can meet with Triumph and Disaster
And treat those two impostors just the same;
If you can bear to hear the truth you've spoken
Twisted by knaves to make a trap for fools,
Or watch the things you gave your life to broken,
And stoop and build 'em up with worn-out tools:

IF you can make one heap of all your winnings
And risk it on one turn of pitch-and-toss,
And lose, and start again at your beginnings
And never breathe a word about your loss;
If you can force your heart and nerve and sinew
To serve your turn long after they are gone,
And so hold on when there is nothing in you
Except the Will which says to them 'Hold on!'

IF you can talk with crowds – and keep your virtue,
Or walk with Kings – nor lose the common touch,
If neither foes nor loving friends can hurt you,
If all men count with you, but none too much
If you can fill the unforgiving minute
With sixty seconds' worth of distance run,
Yours is the Earth and everything that's in it,
And – which is more –
YOU'LL BE A MAN, MY SON!

Margaret Thatcher

5th May 2000

Dear Father Seed,

Thank you for your letter regarding An Anthology of Assurance which you are editing.

Perhaps the most reassuring and inspiring message one could find is contained in the words of the 23rd Psalm. But as I am sure that many people will choose this, may I suggest a verse from *The Island*, a poem by Francis Brett Young.

Yours sincerely

Margaret Thatcher

Father Michael Seed

What are you carrying, Pilgrims, Pilgrims?
What did you carry beyond the sea?
We carried the Book, we carried the Sword,
A steadfast heart in the fear of the Lord,
And a living faith in His plighted word
That all men should be free.

21.5.00

Dear Father Seed,

In reply to your letter of April 7, the following passage has inspired me in times of difficulty. It is from the Bible (King James version), Revelation, Chapter 21, 1-6, particularly these verses:

And I John saw the holy city, new Jerusalem, coming down from God out of heaven, prepared as a bride adorned for her husband.

And I heard a great voice out of heaven saying, Behold, the tabernacle of God *is* with men, and he will dwell with them, and they shall be his people, and God himself shall be with them, *and be* their God.

And God shall wipe away all tears from their eyes; and there shall be no more death, neither sorrow, nor crying, neither shall there be any more pain: for the former things are passed away.

I read this passage aloud at the funeral of a very close friend in 1989 and afterwards wrote a song called "Your funny uncle" which described the funeral and quoted the passage:

And at the end
your funny uncle staring
at all your friends
with military bearing
He stopped to stand
to smile and speak of you directly
"Goodbye", shake hands
like you did everything correctly
to wipe away the tears
No more pain, no fear
no sorrow or dying
no waiting or crying
these former things are passed away
Another life begins today

I wish you success with your book and good causes.

Yours sincerely,

Neil Tennant
Pet Shop Boys

EMORY UNIVERSITY
Candler School of Theology

Atlanta, Georgia 30322

May 10, 2000

Dear Father:

Thank you very much for your letter of April 7, 2000. I trust you had a blessed and happy Easter.

I have myself been very deeply encouraged by certain passages in the Bible, which one could conflate into each other. I cannot get over the wonder of Paul's statement, "Whilst we were yet sinners, Christ died for us." Because God chose me in Christ to be His child, before the foundation of the world, and predestined me to be adopted as one of His children through Jesus Christ. And that, "If God be for us, who can be against us?" For nothing, absolutely nothing can separate us from the love of God in Jesus Christ.

Those are words that speak of how precious I am in the sight of God; loved with a love that will not let me go--with a love that is unchanging and is unchangeable. And that I can do nothing to make God love me more, as I can do nothing to make God love me less. That's wonderful!

God bless you.

Yours sincerely,

Desmond M. Tutu
Archbishop Emeritus
William R. Cannon Visiting Distinguished Professor of Theology

DMT/jls

Prebendary Dr. Chad Varah, CH CBE, MA
Rector
St. Stephen Walbrook

Whitsun Day 2000

Dear Father Michael,

Eye hath not seen, nor ear heard, neither hath entered into the heart of man, the things which God hath prepared for them that love Him. I am not good, but I do love him.

You didn't ask for something to look at, but I'll give you something never failing: The Sculpture of the Burghers of Calais, by Rodin, in Victoria Tower Gardens. The six men of varying ages were ordered by us British besiegers to come out of Calais in their shifts, with halters round their necks, and bearing the keys of the city, to be hanged. They express every human emotion one would expect, and Rodin captures them brilliantly. Queen Philippa pleaded for them and the King reprieved them, but Rodin shows them to us before her intercession.

I go and look at it several times a year.

Yours in O.B.L.,

Chad Varah.

Sir Dennis Walters, MBE

2nd May 2000

Dear Father Michael,

Thank you for your letter of the 7th April. The text I have chosen is the following:

John 20: 19-31

In the evening of that same day, the first day of the week, the doors were closed in the room where the disciples were, for fear of the Jews. Jesus came and stood among them. He said to them, "Peace be with you," and showed them his hands and his side. The disciples were filled with joy when they saw the Lord, and he said to them again, "Peace be with you. As the Father sent me, so am I sending you." After saying this he breathed on them and said: "Receive the Holy Spirit. For those whose sins you forgive, they are forgiven; for those whose sins you retain, they are retained." Thomas, called the Twin, who was one of the Twelve, was not with them when Jesus came. When the disciples said, "We have seen the Lord", he answered, "Unless I see the holes that the nails made in his hands and can put my finger into the holes they made, and unless I can put my hand into his side, I refuse to believe." Eight days later the disciples were in the house again and Thomas was with them. The doors were closed, but Jesus came in and stood among them. "Peace be with you" he said. Then he spoke to Thomas, "Put your finger here: look, here are my hands. Give me your hand; put it into my side. Doubt no longer but believe." Thomas replied, "My Lord and my God!" Jesus said to him: "you believe because you can see me. Happy are those who have not seen and yet believe."

Wishing you every possible success in your charitable enterprise.

Yours sincerely

Dennis Walters

April 9th 2000

Dear Father Seed,
Here is one of my very favourite poems:

I struck the board and cried, No more!
  I will abroad.
What? shall I ever sigh and pine?
  My lines and life are free; free as the road,
  Loose as the winds, as large as store,
  Shall I be still in suit?
  Have I no harvest but a thorn
  To let me blood, and not restore
  What I have lost with cordial fiuit?

Sure there was wine
  Before my sighs did dry it; there was corn
  Before my tears did drown it.
Is the year only lost to me?
  Have I no bays to crown it?
No flowers, no garlands gay? all blasted?
  All wasted?
Not so, my heart; but there is fruit
  And thou hast hands.

Recover all thy sigh-blown age
On double pleasures; leave thy cold dispute
Of what is fit and not; forsake thy cage,
  Thy rope of sands,
Which petty thoughts have made, and made to
    thee
  Good cable, to enforce and draw
  And be thy law,
While thou didst wink and would not see.
  Away; take heed;
  I will abroad.
Call in thy death's head there; tie up thy fears.
  He that forbears
To suit and serve his need,
  Deserves his load.
But as I raved and grew more fierce and wild
  At every word, Methoughts I heard one calling,
  'Child' And I replied, 'My Lord'.

GEORGE HERBERT

With best wishes for the book, and for both
charities,
    yours sincerely,
    Mary Warnock

THE RIGHT HONOURABLE LORD WEATHERILL DL

Dear Michael

9 May 2000

When I was sent away to Boarding School at the age of 7 my Mother gave me a Bible with these words inscribed. In my unhappiness they did not mean much to me then — but later in life they have a comfort and an encouragement.

Warm good wishes for the success of "An Anthology of Assurance"

Bernard Weatherill

Unseen Power that rules and controls our destinies, teach me the symphony of life so that my nature may be in tune with Thine.

Teach me to play life's game with courage, fortitude and confidence.

Endow me with wisdom to guard my tongue and my temper, and to learn with patience the art of ruling my life for its highest good, with due regard for the privacy, rights and limitations of others.

Make me sympathetic in sorrow, realizing that there are hidden woes in every life no matter how exalted or lowly.

Help me to strive for the highest legitimate reward of merit, and opportunity in my activities, but to be ever ready to extend a kindly helping hand to those who need encouragement and succour in their struggle.

If in life's battle I am wounded or tottering, bind my wounds with the balm of hope, and imbue me with courage to arise and continue the strife.

Keep me humble in every relation of life, not unduly egotistical, nor liable to the sin of self-depreciation.

In success keep me modest; and in sorrow, may my soul be uplifted by the thought that if there were no shadow there would be no sunshine.

If I win, crown me with the laurels fitting to be worn by a victor; and if I fail, may it be with my face to the foe fighting manfully.

From: The Rt. Hon. Ann Widdecombe, M.P.

HOUSE OF COMMONS
LONDON SW1A 0AA

25 May 2000

Dear Michael

Thank you very much for your letter of the 3rd May about the publication *An Anthology of Assurance* that you will be editing. Below is the prayer that I turn to most often.

> O Lord God, when thou
> givest to thy servants to
> endeavour any great matter,
> grant us also to know that it
> is not the beginning, but the
> continuing of the same, until
> it be thoroughly finished,
> which yieldeth the true glory.
>
> Prayer based on Words by
> Sir Francis Drake

I do hope the publication will be a huge success.

Yours sincerely,

Ann Widdecombe MP

THE
TABLET

The Tablet Publishing Co. Ltd
Registered in England No. 311249
1 King Street Cloisters
Clifton Walk, London W6 0QZ

From the office of the Editor

Web address: http://www.thetablet.co.uk

Dear Father Michael,

My greatest temptation has been despair. I am better than I was. One turning point came while I was watching birds on the island of Sheppey in the Thames. All day the black devil of depression had sat on my shoulder. But as I saw the clouds of waders turning as one over the water, I thought suddenly, "It is all worth it".

That sense now never leaves me. Faith, hope and love lead us into life. But for those — most of us — afflicted at least some of the time in this way, there is one Bible passage so extraordinary in its reassurance that when I first read it I could hardly believe it:

For if our heart condemn us, God is greater than our heart.

(1 Jn 3:20)

Yours

John

Father Michael Seed,
Franciscan Friars,
St. Francis Friary,
47 Francis St.,
Westminster, London SW1P !QR

14 May 2000.

Dear Fr. Seed,

I am sorry to have been slow in replying to your letter of April 13, but my family has been getting through serial flu, one after the other of us succumbing to the virus. At last we seem to be recovering.

I am not sure the poem I have chosen represents assurance; but it does seem to me to provide a strong sense of the divinity of Jesus Christ to those who might doubt it. It also seems to me to address the modern, sceptical mind much more aptly than do earlier professions of faith. I will leave you to decide whether to include it, and if so, whether also to include the two sentences preceding.

I hope your anthology proves to be a comfort and source of strength to those who read and buy it.

Yours ever,

Shirley Williams

Friday's Child by W. H. Auden
(in memory of Dietrich Bonhoeffer)

He told us we were free to choose
But children as we were, we thought –
'Paternal Love will only use
Force in the last resort

On those too bumptious to repent' –
Accustomed to religious dread,
It never crossed our minds he meant
Exactly what He said.

Perhaps He frowns, perhaps He grieves,
But it seems idle to discuss
If anger or compassion leaves
The bigger bangs to us.

What reverence is rightly paid
To a Divinity so odd
He lets the Adam whom He made
Perform the Acts of God?

It might be jolly if we felt
Awe at this Universal Man
(When kings were local, people knelt);
Some try to, but who can?

The self-observed observing Mind
We meet when we observe at all
Is not alarming or unkind
But utterly banal.

Though instruments at Its command
Make wish and counterwish come true,
It clearly cannot understand
What It can clearly do.

Since the analogies are rot
Our senses based belief upon,
We have no means of learning what
Is really going on,

And must put up with having learned
All proofs or disproofs that we tender
Of His existence are returned
Unopened to the sender.

Now, did He really break the seal
And rise again? We dare not say
But conscious unbelievers feel
Quite sure of Judgement Day.

Meanwhile, a silence on the cross,
As dead as we shall ever be,
Speaks of some total gain or loss,
And you and I are free

To guess from the insulted face
Just what Appearances He saves
By suffering in a public place
A death reserved for slaves.

16th May 2000

Dear Father Michael,

In spite of Rudyard Kipling's quote "If" being very hackneyed,
I still find myself turning to it in hours of need. True, I do so
with a smile, slightly ashamed of being a little childish, but the
magic never fails.

If you can keep your head when all about you
      Are you losing theirs and blaming it on you,
If you can trust yourself when all men doubt you,
      But make allowances for their doubting too:
If you can wait and not be tired of waiting,
      Or being lied about, don't deal in lies,
Or being hated, don't give way to hating,
      And yet don't look too good, nor talk too wise:

If you can dream-and not make dreams your master;
      If you can think-and not make thoughts your aim;
If you can meet with Triumph and Disaster
      And treat those two impostors just the same.

If you can make one heap of all your winnings
  And risk it on one turn of pitch-and-toss,
And loose, and start again at your beginnings
  And never breathe a word about your loss.

If you can talk with crowds and keep your virtue,
  Or walk with Kings-nor loose the common touch,
If neither foes nor loving friends can hurt you,
  If all men count with you, but none too much;

If you can fill the unforgiving minute
  With sixty seconds' worth of distance run,
Yours is the Earth and everything that's in it,
  And-which is more-you'll be a Man, my son!

I bet this text has put more marrow into backbones than any
other.

Yours sincerely

Sir Peregrine Worsthorne

25 April 2000

Dear Father Michael,

Thank you for your letter of 7 April about your new anthology. I would like to
put forward the Prologue to Bertrand Russell's autobiography (published by Allen
and Unwin, 1967).

"Three passions, simple but overwhelmingly strong, have governed my life:
the longing for love, the search for knowledge, and unbearable pity for the suffering of mankind. These passions, like great winds, have blown me hither and
thither, in a wayward course, over a deep ocean of anguish, reaching to the very
verge of despair.

I have sought love, first, because it brings ecstasy - ecstacy so great that
I would often have sacrificed all the rest of life for a few hours of this joy. I
have sought it, next, because it relieves loneliness - that terrible loneliness in
which one shivering consciousness looks over the rim of the world into the cold
unfathomable lifeless abyss. I have sought it, finally, because in the union of
love I have seen, in a mystic miniature, the prefiguring vision of the heaven that
saints and poets have imagined. This is what I sought, and though it might seem
too good for human life, this is what - at last - I have found.

With equal passion I have sought knowledge. I have wished to understand the
hearts of men. I have wished to know why the stars shine. And I have tried to
apprehend the Pythagorean power by which number holds sway above the flux. A little
of this, but not much, I have achieved.

Love and knowledge, so far as they were possible, led upward towards the heavens.
But always pity brought me back to earth. Echoes of cries of pain reverberate in my
heart. Children in famine, victims tortured by opperssors, helpless old people, a
hated burden to their sons, and the whole world of loneliness, poverty and pain
make a mockery of what human life should be. I long to alleviate the evil, but I
cannot, and I too suffer.

This has been my life. I have found it worth living, and would gladly live it
again if the chance were offered me."

I hope this gives you what you want.

Yours sincerely,

Philip Ziegler

Index of Authors

Abd al-Qadir   25
Agate, James   8
Anon   123, 162, 177
Ashwin, Angela   52
Assis, Machadoche de   145
Astley, Sir Jacob   90
Aquinas, St Thomas   78
Auden, W. H.   164, 181

Baghavad-gita   102
Blake, William   58
Breton, Nicolas   99
Byron, Lord   130

Cartland, Barbara   62
Cavafy, Constantin   79
Chekov, Anton   42
Chesterton, G. K.   116
Churchill, W. S.   86
Clough, Arthur, Hugh   45
Coleridge, Mary   59
Common Prayer, Book of   158

David, Elizabeth   69
de Chardin, Teilhard   24, 139
Dickinson, Emily   167
Donne, John   115
Drake, Sir Francis   178

Ecclesiastes   159
Eliot, T. S.   149, 165
Exodus   152

Franklin, Benjamin   111
Fortunatus, Venantius   26

Gibran, Khalil   57
Grenfell, Julian   161
Graves, Robert   83
Gray, Thomas   85

Hammarskjöld, Dag   114
Haskins, Minnie Louise   73
Hemingway, Ernest   130
Herbert, George   72, 106, 176

Hood, Thomas   133
Hopkins, Gerard Manley   31, 75, 97
Hume, Cardinal Basil   21

Ignatius of Loyola, St   7
Inghi   49
Isaiah   127

John, St   63, 175, 179
John Paul II, Pope   20

Kipling, Rudyard   94, 125, 169,
   182
Koran, The   9

Law, William   7
Lao, Tzu   37
Luke, St   44

Marie-Antionette, Queen   108
Mark, St   39
Mass Liturgy, the   131
Matthew, St   67, 163, 166
Milton, John   76
More, Sir Thomas   157

Newman, John Henry   38
Nicholl, Donald   51

O'Donoghue, John   55
Orthodox Liturgy   88

Paul, St   36, 87, 114, 112, 144, 173
Popper, Karl   136
Psalms   23, 74, 113, 129, 153
Pym, Barbara   35

Rix, Brian   147
Russell, Bertrand   184

Sacco, Nicola   41
Salinger, J. D.   140
Shakespeare, William   86
Shelley, P. B.   47
Smith, Sydney   28
Stevenson, R. L.   117

Tennant, Neil   172
Teresa, Mother   20
Teresa of Avila, St   151
Thomas, R. S.   82
Thomas á Kempis, St   21
Thompson, Francis   93
Tonypandy, Lord   132
Toplady, A. M.   91
Traherne, Thomas   65

Valéry, Paul   155

Wilcox, Ella Wheeler   101

Yeats, W. B.   104
Young, Francis Brett   170